1

Options Trading

A Simplified Guide for Beginners with Secrets Strategies to Make Profit Fast! Basics and Tips on How to Trade Options for a Quick Start to your Financial Freedom.

William L. Anderson

By reading this document, the reader agrees that under no circumstances is the author responsible for any losses, direct or indirect, which are incurred as a result of the use of information contained within this document, including, but not limited to, — errors, omissions, or inaccuracies.

INTRODUCTION

Basic Terminologies Used In the Stock Market

What Are Stocks?

Types of Stocks

Common Stocks

Preferred Stocks

Why Do Companies Sell Shares?

What Is The Stock Market?

CHAPTER 1 - OPTIONS TRADING AND THE INDIVIDUAL INVESTOR

How Does The Stock Market Work?

Stock Market Indexes

Bullish and Bearish Markets

Stock Market Corrections and Crash

Analyzing the Stock Market

Fundamental Market Analysis

Technical Market Analysis

Why You Need To Diversify

When to Sell Your Stocks

Why Selling Is So Hard

Is The Company Suffering From Any Setback?

Introduction

Congratulations for buying *Options Trading 1* and thank you for doing so.

Books about the subject flood the market; we thank you for personally picking this one! Efforts were made to make sure all information here is useful. Please enjoy!

Are you eager to jump into the world of investments? Perhaps, you've heard of the benefits and million dollars stories in this seemingly magical world of investments. Slow down, as you risk losing your life's investment in an unfamiliar market. For so many new investors, the world of stocks might look like legalized gambling. They think of scenarios like this: if your stock goes up - you win! If it goes down - you lose! How? You don't know since it has become a game of luck. With this type of mentality, the stock market more or less becomes a game of roulette. However, the more you understand the true nature of stocks, the better you will manage your money.

Therefore, in this chapter, you will learn the basic and common terminologies used in the stock market, the reason why companies sell shares, an in-depth analysis of the mechanics of the stock market, and how to recognize a bearish or bullish market. So, let's start with the basic terminologies you will come across while trading in the stock market.

Basic Terminologies Used In the Stock Market

Shares

In the financial market, shares are a unit of capital that depicts the ownership relationship between the shareholder and the company. In such transactions, investors buy or sell shares through a stockbroker who acts as the middleman. The market value of the shares you buy is determined by the performance of the company and other economic factors such as wars, elections, and new economic policies. In addition to this, dividends are the income you earn from shares.

Bonds

Bonds are an interesting alternative to dividend investments. Bonds are defined as fixed income structures that represent a loan made by an individual investor to a borrower. Most times, the borrower is the government or a corporation. Fixed or variable interests rates are attached to these loans, and the end date is fixed for the payment of the principal to the bond owners. Some investors prefer bonds since they are seen as safe, and can be easily traded with other investors or brokers. Companies or other entities issue bonds to investors when they need to raise money for a new project or re-finance existing debt. They issue bonds that contain the terms and conditions, the time at which the loan (principal) must be paid back, and the interest rates that will be paid. The interest rate is a fixed income that bond owners earn for buying bonds. You should know that the face value or value of bonds differs. In addition to this, you don't have to wait for the bond to expire before you can sell it off.

Equity

In the financial market, the term equity has various definitions. Generally, these definitions revolve around the concept that equity is the difference between the value of assets and liabilities. You can think of equity as the degree of ownership in any asset, once we subtract the cost of the debt associated with it. Here's an example to simplify this term. Imagine you had a car that was worth $15,000, but you owed $5,000 worth of debt against the car. In this case, your equity for the car (asset) was $10,000. Furthermore, equity becomes negative when the cost of liabilities exceeds assets. In terms of shareholder equity or capital, this represents the total number of assets subtracted from liabilities, as divided between shareholders.

Shareholder

You become a shareholder when you own shares of stock in a corporation. Shareholders are the owners of a company since each share of stock they possess entitles them to have a say in the way a corporation operates. However, just because you are a shareholder doesn't mean you can barge in and start firing workers. There are laws in place that protect the company from such actions. Shareholders have the power to elect a board of directors to make major decisions in the company, such as the number of shares to be sold to the public. Besides this, some long-standing corporations pay out dividends to their shareholders.

Initial Public Offering (IPO)

This is a term used to describe the process of a company selling its share of stocks on the stock market for the first time. This is when you hear terms like: "the company is going public". In IPOs, the company's shares are sold to institutional or retail investors, who later sell the investors to others via brokers [WU1]. Investment banks who act as underwriters calculate and establish the value of the company's share, and a detailed overview of the public offering is given to initial investors in the form of a lengthy document known as a prospectus.

Earnings per Share

This is the total profit of the company divided by the number of shares. This is an important factor you must consider before investing in a company. Each part of a company's shares can be likened to pieces of a pie. The larger your share in the corporation, the bigger your pie slices. To know the earnings per share, the investors calculate how much income after-tax each share will receive. Therefore, if a company generates more and more profits annually, but only a little profit makes its way to the shareholders on a per-share basis, then it is considered a terrible investment.

Ticker Symbol

Ticker symbols are used to represent corporations listed on the stock market. They are usually a short group of letters. For instance, Johnson & Johnson has a ticker symbol of JNJ and Coca-Cola has a ticker symbol of KO.

Book Value

This is the total asset of a company that's useful to shareholders. It determines what a shareholder will get in case of liquidation. The book value of a company is calculated as the total asset of a company, excluding the liabilities and intangible assets like patents. Investors can use a corporation's book value to gauge if their stocks are overpriced or undervalued.

Corporations

Here's a term that you will come across countless times in this book - corporations are different from businesses. How? Well, any business that sells shares of stocks to investors needs to first become a corporation. A business must undergo a legal process known as incorporation before it becomes a corporation. It's important to understand that a corporation is different from a sole proprietorship or partnership. In fact, it is a virtual person in the eyes of the law. It is registered with the government and has a federal tax number. More so, a corporation can sue, make contracts, and own properties. There are certain laws put in place to ensure uniformity in the way a corporation operates, and how the public and shareholders are protected. For instance, it is compulsory for every corporation to have a board of directors. The shareholders hold yearly meetings to decide who gets to sit on the board. Shareholders also use corporations as shields against liquidity in case the corporation goes bankrupt.

What Are Stocks?

Also referred to as equities, stocks are issued by companies in a bid to raise capital in order to expand their business operations or take on new projects. To shareholders, stocks represent a claim of ownership on the company's assets or earnings. Your ownership stake becomes higher as you acquire more stocks. You should know, however, that owning stocks does not give you control over the properties of the corporation, as it is protected under laws of ownership. Now that we've got that out of the way, let's take an in-depth look at the different types of stocks companies issue to investors.

Types of Stocks

Companies issue two main types of stocks that get listed on the stock market to their investors. It is important to know the type of stock that you are dealing with since each type of stock comes with its own benefits and setbacks. So, let's get right to it!

Common Stocks

When you hear people talking about stocks, it's very likely that they are referring to common stocks. In fact, common stocks make up a large percentage of the total number of stocks traded on the stock market. A common stock confers voting rights on investors and gives them a client on profits or dividends [WU2]. With common stocks, investors often get one vote per share to elect a board of directors to oversee operations. What's more, these types of stocks come with higher returns than corporate bonds. However, this high return comes with many risks. If a company goes out of business, you stand to lose your entire life's investment (one of the reasons why you need to diversify). If a company goes out of business (bankrupt) and liquidates, common shareholders will not receive their money until bondholders, preferred stockholders, and creditors have been paid.

Preferred Stocks

Preferred stocks have a similar bill function to bonds, and don't usually come with voting rights. Sometimes, some companies offer voting rights with their preferred stocks. With preferred stocks, investors will get a fixed income in the form of dividends. The dividends are guaranteed, unlike common stocks which have variable dividends that are never guaranteed. In fact, many companies don't pay out dividends to common stockholders. Also, in the case of liquidation, preferred shareholders are paid first, before common shareholders. The company settles creditors and bondholders before getting to preferred stockholders.

What's more? Companies can buy back preferred stocks from shareholders at any time. Therefore, you can consider preferred stocks as a blend of the features of bonds and common stocks. Aside from common stocks and preferred stocks, companies can also create classes of shares in a bid to fit the needs of investors. Companies create classes of stocks when they want to keep power concentrated in a certain group of shareholders.

Why Do Companies Sell Shares?

After examining the core terminologies used in the stock market, it is time to take a look at why companies sell their shares, how stocks are issued, and the role of investors in creating a relationship that will benefit both parties. I'm not going to bore you with a vague or uninteresting description. Instead, we will paint a scenario that you can relate to. So, let's use a pizzeria as our case study.

Will has a pizza business with annual earnings of $350,000. His total after-tax profit is $100,000 per year, which is quite a fair amount. However, Will wants more. He wants to expand his business to a neighboring town, which has more potential and a higher population. So, how does he go about this? First, he calculates the cost of building a new pizzeria. The land and equipment required for the new pizzeria will cost up to $500,000 upfront. Then, he has to consider the cost of staff, ingredients for the products, and a delivery vehicle to ensure smooth operation. Right now, Will is looking at a sum of $750,000 to cover all his expenses. He is faced with two options; either getting a loan or going public to get funds from investors like you. On the one hand, he has to consider the interest that comes with loans, and how he could lose everything if he defaults. In addition to this, banks don't always lend money to companies, especially small businesses. Therefore, he makes the decision to give up a percentage of his own control in order to raise cash for his dream. Will invites an underwriter from an investment bank such as JP Morgan or Goldman Sachs to evaluate his total asset, and to set the price for his stocks. As mentioned before, Will's Pizza shop earns $100,000 after-tax profit each year. The company also has a book value of $4 million. Then, the underwriter carries out research and finds out that the average pizza company on the stock market trades for 25 times its company's earnings. Therefore, the underwriter will multiply the company's earnings of $100,000 by 25 and add the book value to the result. This means Will's pizza shop is worth $6.5 million.

Will can decide to sell a certain percentage of his stocks to investors in order to meet his financial target. If he sells 40 percent of his company to the public as stock, this means he gets to keep $3.9 million worth of the business. The underwriters search for investors that will buy the stock, and will ultimately offer Will a check of $2.6 million. With a huge income from sold shares, Will can build not just one but two pizzerias anywhere he wants. On the other hand, investors should expect a minimum profit of at least 10 percent of their investment - it's a win-win for both parties!

This is a scenario that depicts the mutual relationship between shareholders and corporations. Now that we have got that out of the way, let's delve into the basics of the stock market and how to understand its technicalities.

What Is The Stock Market?

The stock market is not like your neighborhood grocery store: you can only buy and sell through licensed brokers who make trades on major indexes like NASDAQ and S&P 100. This is where investors meet up to buy and sell stocks or other financial investments like bonds. The stock market is made up of so many exchanges, like the NASDAQ or the New York Exchange. These exchanges are not open all through the day. Most exchanges like the NASDAQ and NYSE are open from 9:30 am to 4 pm. EST. Although premarket and trading after closing time now exist, not all brokers do this.

Companies list their stocks on an exchange in a bid to raise money for their business, and investors buy those shares. In addition to this, investors can trade shares among themselves, and the exchange keeps track of the rate of supply and demand of each listed stock. The rate of supply and demand for stocks determines the price. If there's a high demand for a particular stock, its price tends to rise. On the other hand, the price of a stock goes down when there's less demand for it. The stock market computer algorithm handles these varying fluctuations in prices.

Chapter 1 - Options Trading and the Individual Investor

This chapter looks at the setups for profitable trades - to get a rough overview and to see where the market is in general development. Then we turn to the technical tools to find an entry point, stop-fall protection, if you're wrong, and the likely candidates for the price moves. As in the real estate business, trading is the most important factor: the location, the location, the location. Then there is the timing, the timing, the timing. The setup gives you a rough overview of the market's current state of development - key information when looking for short-term reversal or confirmation patterns. Ideally, you open your position in the area where the likelihood of success is greatest.

How Does The Stock Market Work?

A Stock market analysis definitely looks like gibberish to beginners and average investors. However, you should know that the way this market works is actually quite simple. Just imagine a typical auction house or an online auction website. This market works in the same way - it allows buyers and sellers to negotiate prices and carry out successful trades. The first stock market took place in a physical marketplace, however, these days, trades happen electronically via the internet and online stockbrokers. From the comfort of your homes, you can easily bid and negotiate for the prices of stocks with online stockbrokers.

Furthermore, you might come across news headlines that say the stock market has crashed or gone up. Once again, don't fret or get all excited when you come across such news. Most often than not, this means a stock market index has gone up or down. In other words, the stocks in a market index have gone down. Before we proceed, let's explore the meaning of market indexes.

Stock Market Indexes

As mentioned earlier, when people refer to the rise and fall of the stock market, they are generally referring to one of the major stock market's market indexes. Market indexes track the performance of a group of stocks in a particular sector like manufacturing or technology. The value of the stocks featured in an index is representative of all the stocks in that sector. It is very important to take note of what stocks each market index represents. As mentioned in the first chapter, you should invest in a niche you are comfortable with. In addition to this, giant market indexes like the Dow Jones Industrial Average, the NASDAQ composite, and the Standard & Poor's 500, are often used as proxies for the performance of the stock market as a whole. You can choose to invest in an entire index through the exchange-traded funds and index funds, as it can track a specific sector or index of the stock market.

Bullish and Bearish Markets

Talking about the bullish outlook of the stock market is guaranteed to get beginners looking astonished. Yes, it sounds ridiculous at first, but with time, you get to appreciate the ingenuity of these descriptions. Let's start with the bearish market. A bear is an animal you would never want to meet on a hike; it strikes fear into your heart, and that's the effect you will get from a bearish market. A bear market depicts when stock prices are falling across several of the indexes mentioned earlier. The threshold for a bearish market varies within a 20 percent loss or more.

Most young investors unfamiliar with a bear market as we've been in a bull market since the first quarter of 2019. In fact, this makes it the second-longest bull market in history. Just as you have probably guessed by now, a bull market indicates that stock prices are rising. You should know that the market is continually changing from bull to bear and vice versa. From the Great Recession to the global market crash, these changing market prices indicate the start of larger economic patterns. For instance, a bull market shows that investors are investing heavily and that the economy is doing extremely well. On the other hand, a bear market shows investors are scared and pulling back, with the economy on the brink of collapsing. If this made you paranoid about the next bear market, don't fret. Business analysts have shown that the average bull market generally outlasts the average bear market by a large margin. This is why you can grow your money in stocks over an extended period of time.

Stock Market Corrections and Crash

A stock market crash is every investor's nightmare. It is usually extremely difficult to watch stocks that you've spent so many years accumulating diminish before your very eyes. Yes, this is how volatile the stock market is. Stock market crashes usually include a very sudden and sharp drop in stock prices, and it might herald the beginning of a bear market. On the other hand, stock market corrections occur when the market drops by 10 percent - this is just the market's way of balancing itself. The current bull market has gone through 5 market corrections.

Analyzing the Stock Market

You are not psychic. It is nearly impossible to accurately predict the outcome of your stock to the last detail. However, you can become near perfect at reading the stock market by learning how to properly analyze the components of this market. There are two basic types of analyses: technical analysis and fundamental analysis.

Fundamental Market Analysis

Fundamental analysis involves getting data about a company's stocks or a particular sector in the stock market, via financial records, company assets, economic reports, and market share. Analysts and investors can conduct fundamental analysis via the metrics on a corporation's financial statement. These metrics include cash flow statements, balance sheet statements, footnotes, and income statements. Most times, you can get a company's financial statement through a 10-k report in the database. In addition to this, the SEC's EDGAR is a good place to get the financial statement of the company you are interested in. With the financial statement, you can deduce the revenues, expenses, and profits a company has made.

What's more? By looking at the financial statement, you will have a measure of a company's growth trajectory, leverage, liquidity, and solvency. Analysts utilize different ratios to make an accurate prediction about stocks. For example, the quick ratio and current ratio are useful in determining if a company will be able to pay its short-term liabilities with the current asset. If the current ratio is less than 1, the company is in poor financial health and may not be able to recover from its short-term debt. Here's another example: a stock analyst can use the debt ratio to measure the current level of debt taken on by the company. If the debt ratio is above 1, it means the company has more debt than assets and it's only a matter of time before it goes under.

Technical Market Analysis

This is the second part of stock market analysis and it revolves around studying past market actions to predict the stock price direction. Technical analysts put more focus on the price and volume of shares. Additionally, they analyze the market as a whole and study the supply and demand factors that dictate market movement. In technical analyses, charts are of inestimable value. Charts are a vital tool as they show the graphical representation of a stock's trend within a set time frame. What's more? Technical investors are able to identify and mark certain areas as resistance or support levels on a chart. The resistance level is a previous high stock price before the current price. On the other hand, support levels are represented by a previous low before the current stock price. Therefore, a break below the support levels marks the beginning of a bearish trend. Alternatively, a break above the resistance level marks the beginning of a bullish market trend. Technical analysis is only effective when the rise and fall of stock prices are influenced by supply and demand forces. However, technical analysis is mostly rendered ineffective in the face of outside forces that affect stock prices such as stock splits, dividend announcements, scandals, changes in management, mergers, and so on. Investors can make use of both types of analyses to get an accurate prediction of their stock values.

Why You Need To Diversify

According to research by Ned Davis, a bear market occurs every 3.5 years and has an average lifespan of 15 months. One thing is clear, though: you can't avoid bear markets. You can, however, avoid the risks that come with investing in a single investment portfolio. Let's look at a common mistake that new investors typically make. Research points to the fact that individual stocks dwindle to a loss of 100 percent. By throwing in your lot with one company, you are exposing yourself to many setbacks. For example, you can lose your money if a corporation is embroiled in a scandal, poor leadership, and regulatory issues. So, how can you balance out your losses? By investing in the aforementioned index fund or ETF fund, as these indexes hold many different stocks, as by doing this, you've automatically diversified your investment. Here's a nugget to cherish: put 90 percent of your investment funds in an index fund, and put the remaining 10 percent in an individual stock that you trust.

When to Sell Your Stocks

One thing is sure - you are not going to hold your stocks forever. All our investment advice and energies are directed towards buying. Yes, it is the buying of stocks that kick-start the whole investment when chasing your dream concept. However, just as every beginning has an end, you will eventually sell every stock you buy. It is the natural order. Even so, selling off stock is not an easy decision. Heck! It's even harder to determine the right time to sell. This is the point where greed and human emotions start to battle with pragmatism. Many investors try to make sensible selling decisions solely based on price movements. However, this is not a sure strategy, as it is still sensible to hold onto a stock that has fallen in value. Conversely, selling a stock when it has reached your target is seen as prudent. So, how can you navigate around this dilemma? Before touching on other parts in this section, let's first tackle the reason why selling is so hard.

Why Selling Is So Hard

Do you know why it's so hard to let go of your stocks even when you have a fixed strategy to follow? The answer lies in human greed. When making decisions, it's an innate human tendency to be greedy. Here's an example: An investor purchases shares at $30, and tells herself that when the stocks hit $40, she will sell. Here comes an all-too-familiar trend - when the stocks finally hit $40, the investor will hold out and see if her stock prices will rise beyond $40. You can see that human nature is already creeping in. Surely, the stocks hit $45, and greed takes over logical thinking. She decides to wait to see if it rises beyond $45. Suddenly, the stock prices plummet down to $36. At this point, she tells herself that once the stocks rise again to $40, she will sell. Unfortunately, this never happens. This stock continues to plummet down to $25. Finally, she succumbs to her frustrations and sells at $25.

From the above example, you can see how greed and irrationality took over her sound investment plan. In this scenario, sound investment plans were replaced with gambling tendencies. Although the investment was a loss at $5 per share, her true loss stands at $20 per share. This is because she had the opportunity to sell at $45 but she held out, hoping for even higher prices. Knowing when to sell is truly a paramount factor. Sometimes, a good selling decision that brings some profits to your table might look like a poor selling decision. However, in this scenario, it's advised to say prudent. To remove human emotions from your decisions, you can consider adding a limit order which automatically locks in your selling decision. The limit order will sell once it reaches your target price.

Wait! Ask Yourself These Questions before Selling Your Shares
You have held out long enough, and you feel it's time to take the big leap. Perhaps, you have seen the haphazard rise and fall of

stock prices, and you don't want to be at the short end of the stick. Hold on! Ask yourself these questions before you sell.

Is The Company Suffering From Any Setback?

These days we have access to a lot more information than we ever had. As you have nonstop access to the internet, it can be extremely difficult not to constantly check market data. However, beware that doing this can make you succumb to emotional triggers, and this might ultimately lead to poor selling decisions. The best thing you can do in this situation is to get some perspective. Compare the company's total revenues to its benchmark and to others in the same sector. This can help you to discern if the slow performance is an indication of falling stock prices or just a random market movement.

Is Your Portfolio Out Of Balance?

As an ideal investor, you have diversified your investment across various sectors. Over time, some stocks begin to perform better than others in that portfolio, making your investments shift towards the out-performers. Therefore, it is necessary to bring your investments back in line to conform to your fixed asset plan. In this situation, you are faced with two options to even the scales: you either buy more of the stocks that have fallen behind or sell the outperforming stocks.

Will You Get A Tax Break?

Yes, your investments have reached your target price and you can wait to sell. Before you do, remember that selling a stock that has increased in a tax-prone brokerage account can trigger a tax bill. The rate of the tax depends on whether you have held the investment for more than a year. If you have, you are eligible for a reduced long-term capital tax rate. If not, you will attract higher short-term tax rates.

Is There A Better Investment For Your Money?

According to billionaire investor and guru, Warren Buffet, the best holding time is forever. However, that's pretty unrealistic for an investor with a finite income. Sometimes, we sell off investments in order to meet up with certain needs such as retirement, college funds, vacations, and anything else that requires capital. Admittedly, it's a wise choice to sell off stocks to meet up with current cash needs and to avoid the volatility of the market. However, I advise not to use your long-term funds for your immediate needs.

How Will You Make Your Exit?

Once again, you are not psychic. It is nearly impossible to time a perfect sale - you don't know when a stock is at its lowest point or when it's at its highest point. Running to sell off your stocks can save you from losing more, and it also denies you the opportunity to gain additional income if the stock rises. Those are the uncertainties that you have to deal with as an investor. However, there's a trick to selling your shares. You can sell shares at different time periods. If you sell them all at once, you might lose out on additional opportunities. If the stock has good potential, then you should sell part of it and hold on to the rest.

Becoming a Super Investor

Every day, you come across internet ads and brokers promising to make you a "super" investor. You must come across a few of these adverts every week. It's a pity that many jumps on this bandwagon of investment without learning how to properly navigate the world of stocks. The word, "investor" has been bandied around so many times that it has lost its value. It is therefore not surprising to see some lose their life fortune all in the name of investment. Investing your money allows you to build wealth. More so, it involves putting your money in areas that have the potential to create huge returns. You really deserve to accomplish your dreams. However, if you are still undecided about investing or not, here are a few reasons to get you on board.

Why You Need To Invest

Here's another question for you: How would you feel on retirement day if your friend or work buddy was sitting on a million-dollar investment, and you weren't? Regret? Pain?

Disappointment? Depression? These negative emotions will definitely crop up in the future unless you take the necessary steps against this.

Save For Retirement

The government retirement funds just aren't enough to meet your future needs. There is plenty of uncertainty surrounding the future, and it is wise to safeguard it. You can invest your retirement savings into investment portfolios, such as bonds, real estate, stocks, and precious metals. So, you can comfortably live off funds earned from investments when it's time to retire. Here's another angle to this: you can earn a continuous income every month or annually by investing your retirement savings in dividend stocks. You can also re-invest income from dividends into more stocks. Wait! Don't let me spill the beans just yet. I will explain all the principles of dividend investments in the next chapter.

Earn Higher Income

Well, this part is obvious. What's the essence of investing if you can't achieve your financial goals? However, this part is quite tricky as not all stocks are worth investing in. The stock market appreciation can remain stagnant for years. A typical example is the Dow Jones, which remained stagnant for 17 years. The Dow Jones is one of the oldest running US market index. This market index reached 995 in January 1966 and it did not surpass the 995 price level until December 1982. Now, imagine if you had invested in this index. This means your investment portfolio was stagnant for 17 years, with no appreciation at all. Therefore, always invest in stocks that will guarantee a continuous income despite the upheavals of the stock market.

Reduce Taxable Income

This is a win-win situation. First, you get to invest and at the same time, you reduce your taxable income. By putting part of your pre-tax income into an investment plan, you will save more money. In addition to this, if you incur a loss from an investment, you may apply that loss against any profit from other investments, and this lowers the amount of your taxable income.

Help Businesses to Grow

No matter how small you invest, your money can make a huge impact on an ailing business. Investing is about more than just gaining profit, it involves backing new ventures with the potential of creating cutting-edge products. Ultimately, you are building a future for yourself and the businesses you invest in.

How Much Money Should You Invest?

How much should I save and put into my investment portfolio? This question has always been on the lips of new investors. Although it's a straightforward question, its answer has always eluded many. Since there's no clear-cut rule on how much you need to invest, most investors often save or invest lower and this can affect their long-term financial goals. Before we proceed, it is important to know the difference between savings and investments.

Difference between Savings and Investments

Fact is, many investors don't know that savings and investments are two completely different entities that play different roles, and have different functions. So, before you set out on the journey to building wealth through passive income, you need to understand these concepts.

Savings is the process of storing cold hard cash in an extremely safe yet liquid account. Liquid, in this context, means that it's stored in a place that allows you to easily access your cash within a short time frame. These include savings accounts supported by the FDIC, checking accounts, and treasury bills. Some savings accounts come with interest rates, but these are usually too small to create a passive income. Many investors including those who lived through the Great Depression recommend keeping a store of cold hard cash in case of a meltdown or market crash.

Investments, on the other hand, is the process of using your capital to procure an asset that you think has a good chance of generating an acceptable income during the course of your investment. You are reading this book to learn how to invest due to the promise of a continuous source of income. You should know that there are many factors that threaten your investment, and a single mistake can wipe out part of your investment portfolio, or even worse, wipe it out in its entirety.

Before you embark on a journey of becoming a super investor, it is necessary to save. Think of savings as a foundation upon which you build your financial structures. You should know that your savings are what provide you with the capital for your investments. Those who don't save are likely to sell off their investments in hard times, and this is not a recipe for getting rich. Therefore, as a general rule, you ought to save an amount that's sufficient to cover all your personal expenses, including your mortgage and utility bills for a span of six months.

Questions to Help You Determine How Much You Want To Invest

First, start by asking yourself these questions, which will help you to arrive at your answer.

How much passive income do I want to earn from my investments? Perhaps you want enough passive income to buy a new house or pay off your mortgage. While trying to arrive at your desired figure, take into account the price of the things you want and the cost of upkeep.

How Much Tolerance Do I Have?

In other words, how high is your risk tolerance? Can you tolerate watching your investment value move wildly up and down? The quicker you want to reach your target financial goals, the bigger the fluctuation in your investment value. Sometimes, you may have to watch your accounts go up by 50 percent or go down by 70 percent.

When Do I Need To Access The Money?

This question is vital, especially when you are using tax-deferred accounts like 401[k] or Roth IRA. You can invite heavy penalties and taxes if you withdraw your money from these accounts before the age of 59. Furthermore, you need to calculate the number of years you want to build up your portfolio for in order to increase the compound interest rates.

Are You Willing To Sacrifice Your Current Standard of Living For Your Dreams?

The Answer

Now, let's look at how we can provide an answer to the main question: how much should you invest? I would say that you already have a fair idea of how you want to live in the future. Perhaps, you have picked your dream house, car, or holiday on an exotic island. Or, you have calculated the sufficient amount for your kids' college fees? Now that you have those images in mind, ask yourself this: how much money do I need to achieve this and live the way I want? Would it take $10,000 per year? Perhaps it would take $150,000. Calculate your total income per year and divide it by 0.4 to discover the assets it would require to back that level of annual income. The next thing you need to figure out is how soon you need the money. Let's say you are 30 and you plan to retire by the age of 60. That gives you 30 years of continuous savings. By increasing the amount you save every month, you effectively reduce the number of years needed to reach your financial target. Mind you, do not take this to the extreme. Money solely exists for you to create opportunities for your loved ones and lead a better lifestyle. Don't overdo it!

Adopting the Traits of Super Investors

Successful investors have certain traits in common, irrespective of their investment portfolios. Whether you earn a tidy sum every month from invest incomes and dividends, or you are a financial genius with a laudable portfolio of high investment returns, these traits will ensure that you stay afloat the uncertainties of the financial market. So, before you jump on to the notion of becoming an investor, you need to adopt certain traits to survive the financial market.

Acquire the Right Temperament

Yes, having the right temperament can make a lot of difference in the financial world. Mind you, this has nothing to do with discernment, intelligence or wisdom. It simply means developing the right attitude. For instance, patience is a strong trait you need to develop, as you should understand that some things take time. As I mentioned earlier, investing is not a get-rich-quick scheme. Your investment will not magically turn into a huge sum overnight. Heck, you will hardly see the result of your investment in the first few years.

In addition to exercising patience, learn to stay away from the crowd. Yes, you must be willing to stick to a plan while ignoring the will of the crowd. This brings to mind the 1990's dot.com bubble when some of the world's best investors refused to be swayed by public opinion. These super investors recognized that bubbles don't last. So, you should know that not every stock or asset is worth investing in. Some investors stick to earning dividends, rents, and interest incomes in order to avoid the uncertainties of the stock market.

Lastly, don't get too emotional. In fact, you will hardly reach your financial goal if you are clouded by emotions. Learn to separate market fluctuations from the inherent value of your assets. For example, let's say you bought an apartment building that nets you $100,000 per year in passive income, and someone comes around and offers to buy the building for $200,000 – you would probably laugh in their face since you know the inherent value of the building.

Learn the ropes! There's no shortcut or cheat for this method. It is vital for you to know how to calculate the intrinsic value of your assets, and this includes getting familiar with the terms, regulations, and laws of investment. It doesn't matter if it's a government bond, a share of stock or a car wash business; you will be at a disadvantage if you don't know to pull out a calculator and punch in the figures yourself. Yes, the calculations involved looking daunting or impossible. However, don't lose heart. All you have to do is to continually ask yourself this question - "how much do I have to pay for a dollar of net present earnings?". Your net present earning is the difference between the current value of your cash inflow and the current value of your outflows. By asking yourself this question over and over again, you will notice your thoughts becoming clearer. In fact, it will help you to sieve genuine and high returns from shady investments. Remember, it only takes a few good financial decisions to reach your desired target.

Understand the Risks Involved

You need to understand that the market won't be rosy all the time. The market isn't fallible. Heck! Stock prices went down when the New York Stock Exchange was shut down for 136 days during World War I. During this long hiatus, investors counting on capital appreciation from their stocks were disappointed. However, those with dividend stocks kept on receiving their paychecks. So, it is important to place your eggs in the right basket.

You should also keep track of trends and the financial history of the stock you are investing in. In fact, you need to have a firm grip on your financial history in order to build your net worth and manage your money. If you take a look at the Dutch Tulip Bubble, the dot.com bubble, and the real estate bubble, you can see that there isn't much difference between them. Therefore, by arming yourself with these turning points in history, you get to delve into the psychology that influences the selling and buying decisions of individuals. This will help you to avoid financial mistakes that will haunt you and your loved ones. Additionally, mental models are an important tool that you can use to avoid mistakes. In the following chapters, I will show you the strategies you can employ to succeed in investments.

Understand Your Investments

Do you know that stock funds are different from bond funds, and a stock index fund is not the same as stock? Most people are generally unaware of the different terms and regulations of investing in the stock market. It is probably not a surprise that Warren Buffet, billionaire and investment guru, made it a rule to never invest in what he does not understand. In other words, it is risky to invest in a niche that's difficult to explain. It's no surprise, then, that Buffet has steered clear of investing heavily in the tech industry. Books are also an excellent way to get information on the stocks you are interested in. Yes, I love the internet and its array of free information; however, nothing beats a good book when you want in-depth knowledge on a particular subject.

The Ultimate Timing for All Markets

Short-term trades that did not perform well or that I did not get out in time became my long-term investments. Maybe you have heard this before: "We all know that things have to go up again." I would like to assure you that the market has nothing to do. But if I had to say exactly when and at which price the market will turn around again, then certainly just when I close my position and not a minute earlier. Get to know this principle well, because it will save you a lot of money. It has already brought me a lot of money. Investors often called me in the hope that I would support them on the assumption that the market in which they were invested would soon recover. My answer is always the same: "Get me to know when you get off, then I will buy." If a position does not perform well, get off. Do not cling to positions. Then you still have enough capital for the next trade. Learn to love the small losses.

The Technology Revolution

The average security holder can now easily check these formulas using cost-effective software package. Nevertheless, the promise of fast wealth is always tempting even for the best. But the philosopher's stone just does not exist. If it existed, then surely someone would have won everything for a long time, and we would have no more markets. But you can work out a technical advantage by studying charts, and you also have to control your psyche. Some people could not even make money by giving them a copy of the Wall Street Journal. And this, you should realize yourself.

A successful trader needs to have knowledge. But possessing knowledge does not necessarily make you a successful trader. The knowledge and the successful trader are separated by a gigantic divide. Few of us can jump over this gap, and those who make it must be very careful not to rush back into the abyss. Once you have reached a certain level of wealth, accumulating more things will increase neither your satisfaction nor your freedom. Trading has the potential of being truly enjoyable, but like overdoing anything else, it can become an addiction.

The Stages of the Price Movement

All speculative markets go through the following stages of price movement:

1.   Accumulation (Congestion) - The low of the market
2.   Rise or breakout
3.   Distribution (Congestion) - The high of the market
4.   Waste or burglary

The fundamental understanding of these different stages of the market movement is essential for successful traders. Approximately 85% of the time the market is in a phase of congestion during which you should settle for modest gains. We will look at different market phases to see the different stages and know when to make a quick profit in a congestion phase or benefit from a breakout or break-in. First, look at the market situation in a rough overview and look for favorable opportunities. You usually use a chart set for a longer timeframe. Then your analysis is finely tuned with the observation of a shorter-term chart. So, you'll find out when to board, when to take profits, and perhaps most importantly, when to leave the sinking ship because you're on the wrong side of the trade. When looking closely at bar charts, it often becomes clear which direction will be most likely for the course. A chart contains a lot of information: if the demand exceeds the bid, then the price rises until a balance is established. The chart is also a reflection of fear and greed.

• Greed: "If only I had bought more, I could have made millions."
• Fear: "Man, if the course continues to break, then I lose everything I have!"

Fear is the stronger of the two emotions, so markets fall faster than they rise. After a breakout or collapse, the market may enter a phase of re-accumulation or re-distribution. This is where Newton's theory comes in: a moving body tends to move on. This means that once a trend has begun, it tends to continue with periodically recurring periods of interruption or rest. The basic wave theory with the five main waves up or down deals with this type of course movement. As a result, price action usually continues after a period of consolidation in the original direction. If the evidence is not reversed by important chart information, then you should trade in the same direction the course was before the congestion. Be wary of reversals after the second or third rest period during a break or break.

Although these patterns may differ in detail, they still repeat themselves in all securities markets. Some stocks were trapped for years in congestion phases. These were mostly the bad fundamentals that mostly stay there.

Setup for Accumulation

Phase 1 - The Peak Of Sales

Accumulation setup usually begins with a peak of sales. This is the first sign of the fatigue of the decline and the beginning of accumulation. The last bar shows the largest span with strongly increasing volumes.

The sales peak is followed by a sharp rise in prices. This price rally exceeds every step down in the previous move down both in terms of time and price. This is a prerequisite for the transition of the market into the accumulation phase. Without this sharp rally, you cannot say whether the downtrend is over or not.

This rapid increase in price is followed by a test of the previous lowest price. This movement either turns up early or leads to a new, slightly deeper low.

Phase 2 - Support and Resistance

Now the market is entering a phase in which supply and demand are more or less balanced. Here are the areas of support and resistance. The range of support is the range of the lowest bar of a sell peak or a succeeding low. The area of resistance is the exact opposite: accumulation lows on positive days increase slightly and become weaker on negative days. Towards the end of this phase, the tops and bottoms will be higher than previous rallies and reactions.

After a sharp rise in prices, there will be several price declines followed by significant rallies. After two or three unsuccessful attempts to reach a new low, you should pay more attention to positive bars with a large span. These indicate that each approach to these lows will buy heavily. The third time points to a very high probability that the market will break out. A tendency towards a rally towards the end of accumulation is likely. A potential entry point for purchase is the second or third brief collapse in accumulation.

The term "clear" means that the rise exceeds the earlier tops by at least an average length of the curve. The extent of exceeding one or more earlier tops indicates the completion of the accumulation phase. If earlier tops are broken only timidly, and the price falls back quickly, then we go from sufficient supply and a possible relapse into the deeper areas of support.

Conversely, a significant breakthrough with further subsequent increases implies continued demand. Additional confirmation is given by a course that lasts several bars long over these previous tops. From this, we conclude that the accumulation is complete and that there is likely to be an increase.

After the signs of strength, the price generally corrects to about 50% of the previous price movement. This marks the beginning of the rising phase. Resist the urge to buy when the price reaches new heights. Often, these are impulsive buyers who are afraid of not being present at the big breakout. But there are countless other stocks that are just at the end of the accumulation phase just before the outbreak is up. Open your positions on your terms and do not chase after the course. If you chase the course and buy on the top, you are often stopped out by normal course corrections.

Brief summary:
1. The first rise after a peak in sales rarely lasts.
2. If you buy in the early stages of accumulation, then small gains are likely until the end of accumulation.
3. The best odds are when you buy towards the end of the accumulation phase.
4. The biggest gains are made during the rise and break-up phases.

If the congestion phase of the course becomes obvious, then the good points for profit taking are in the area of resistance. Sell orders should be placed early enough, as these areas are often only reached very briefly before the price falls again. The profit opportunity can be over quickly when the target price is reached, and the order is not. It's a wrong thing to wait and check what the course does when it enters the resistance zone. Watching a shorter timeframe can be helpful.

Last Market Adjustment

At the end of accumulation, a final market adjustment may occur. This shows up as a sudden slump in the course below the total accumulation area with increased volume. This is followed by an equally rapid increase, which makes up for the whole loss. Then often comes a short drop in price, which reverses quickly and increases again with high volume and strong thrust. The latest market adjustment is trapping the traders who sell at a new low. These trades can quickly lead to large losses. This price movement is also called V-bottom.

Setup for the Distribution

Phase 1 - The Peak of the Purchases

The setup for distribution usually begins with a purport. This is the first sign of the fatigue of the price rise and the beginning of the distribution.

On the heels of the sale follows a sharp price slump. This price decline exceeds every step up in the previous uptrend, both in terms of time and price. This is a prerequisite for the transition of the market into the distribution phase. Without this sharp decline, one cannot say whether the uptrend is over or not. This rapid rate of decline is followed by a test of the previous highest price. This movement can either turn back down early or lead to a new, slightly higher high.

Phase 2 - Support and Resistance

Now the market is entering a phase in which supply and demand are more or less balanced. During distribution, the volume will increase a bit on negative days and on positive days will be weaker.

After a sharp price collapse, there will be several price increases followed by significant reactions. After two or three unsuccessful attempts to reach a new high, you should pay more attention to negative bars with large margins. These indicate that each time you approach these high points, you are selling heavily. The third time points to a very high probability that the market will break down. A tendency towards a rally towards the end of accumulation is likely.

The term "significant" means that the waste falls below the previous bottoms by at least an average bar length. The extent of under-run of one or more previous bottoms indicates the completion of the distribution phase. If earlier bottoms are broken only tentatively and the price rises quickly again, then we assume sufficient demand and a possible relapse into the higher areas of resistance. Additional confirmation is given by a course that stays several bars below these earlier bottoms. From this, we conclude that the distribution is complete and that price collapse is likely.

After the sign of weakness, the price usually corrects to about 50% of the previous price movement. This marks the beginning of the break-in phase. Resist the urge to sell when the price drops to new depths. Often, these are impulsive buyers who are afraid of not being there when the price plummets. However, there are countless other stocks that are just at the end of the distribution phase just before the outbreak down. Open your positions on your terms and do not chase the course. If you chase the course and sell on the bottom, you are often stopped out by normal course corrections.

If the distribution phase of the course becomes obvious, then the good points for profit taking are in the area of support. This area is located in the area around the former bottoms of the Congestion. Sales orders need to be placed in advance, as the profitable ranges are often reached only very briefly before the price rises again. The profit opportunity can be over quickly when the target price is reached, and the order is not. When the course enters the support zone, waiting is dangerous. Watching a shorter timeframe can be helpful.

Re-Accumulation

Trading securities would be easy if one could always assume that a peak of buying follows a phase of distribution followed by a downward movement. In reality, of course, that looks different. The course is entering a congestion phase, but it can also be a re-accumulation. Everything can point to an imminent price decline after a buying trip. But that does not mean that the course is sure to break. It can also be a period of rest during which the powers of supply and demand decide which direction to continue. The course can often go through several rallies and reactions. After the second or third rally in this congestion phase, the span and the position of the bars in the course area often indicate the direction of the next move. As a rule, after a congestion phase, the courses maintain the direction they had been following before the congestion. If a stock that moves into a congestion phase after a buying spike and if you trade at all in this congestion phase, then you should sell up to the gradual slope flattening and buy at bottoms. Note that the lows are higher and the price for some bars is in the upper range of the price range. This indicates a re-accumulation with a probable further price increase. In the case of re-distribution, the opposite is true in the opposite case.

The Phases of the Rise and Burglary

The stages of increase and burglary are the most promising. However, these price movements account for only about 15% between the successive congestions. The theory of parallel motion excels at fast markets. Basically, this theory states that rallies and reactions correspond to previous rallies and reactions. Buy at the same levels of reaction and take your winnings in equal rallies or spurts. The break-in phase is the approximate mirror image of the rising phase. The course usually falls faster and deeper than it rises. After all, fear is a stronger feeling than greed.

The Exhaustion of the Course

After a long climb or even three consecutive bars in one direction, prices are often in the most critical situation, which can lead to correction and the beginning of a new trend. A strong reversal bar in such situations is a good indication that one should worry about a short position. Close the position again if the price does not really break in the next few days. A lower opening price is one of the first signs of fatigue and perhaps the end of the movement.

Five indications that a rising price is going into a congestion phase:

1. The course forms two negative bars with a large spread.

2. The price does not reach a new high over a period of ten bars.

3. The course has non-overlapping days that are opposite to the trend. A non-intersecting bar is a bar whose upper end is below the lower peak of the previous bar. This can occur three or four bars after the highest bar.

4. The course shows a sharp kink or a jump after a steady rise. The drawback is that the price drops to a new low, does not find an offer and then rises aggressively. The jump occurs when the price suddenly rises to a new high, finds no demand, and quickly falls back.

5. The course goes back 75% or more of the last move.

The End of the Movement

The end of the price movement is displayed if the existing high of the movement cannot be broken up with three attempts and no new high forms. Here profits are taken, or the stops are set closer.

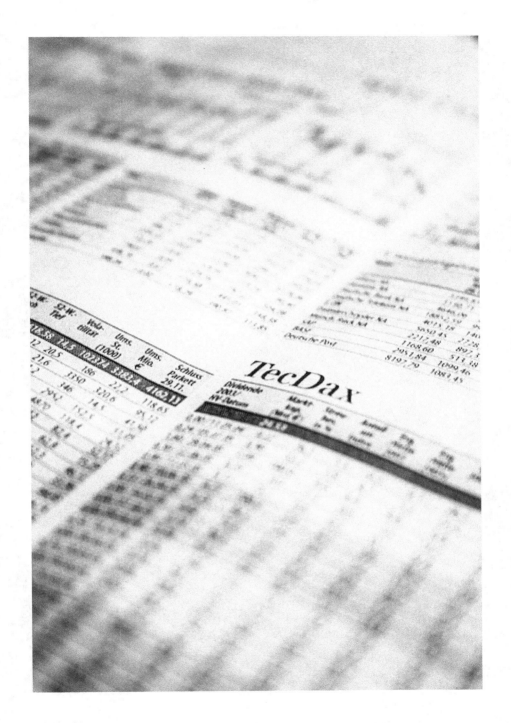

Chapter 2 - Understanding Options

The big question is: how do you apply your skills to make money on the stock market? Before you finish reading this book, you will get some answers. You need to see the patterns and setups as they appear, not just after that - anyone can see them afterward. This is followed by a possible application method. Rules are created. Charts show patterns and the locations where the rules for determining entry and exit points should be applied.

Determine whether the congestion is a re-accumulation or re-distribution based on the last increase or break. Assume this until the congestion pattern tells you otherwise.

The Stop

We propose two steps: an average spread below the last reaction low or the span of the entry bar below the entry bar. Once we have some freedom of movement, the stop will be tightened. Close the position if the price does not behave within three bars. Then do not wait until the stop is triggered.

Trade or Not?

You do not risk your capital if you are not invested in the market. This trading style limits exposure to approximately 10% to 15% of the total observation period. Between 85% and 90% of the time, you are not in the market. During an accumulation or distribution phase, a position can be held. Although there is nothing wrong with this approach, it involves the risk of losing significant portions of the profits. The pattern may be distribution rather than accumulation. You need to study many charts until you find that this approach is workable and fits your trading style. This approach requires a lot of judgment. They should try to automate as many rules as possible to minimize uncertainty.

Trade High-Value Assets

Active trading is best suited for the stocks and/or futures that are moving or in trend phases, and not the boring ones like the securities that are constantly going sideways. The definition of a value that moves is quite subjective. Many sources cite lists of securities that outperform and outperform others, and one of the best is Investor's Business Daily.

Moving securities may have the following characteristics:
- Increased volatility
- Reaching a new four-week high
- Securities in the rising phase

- Significantly upwards or downwards inclined sliding average of the last 20 days
- The leading values in a specific market segment

Brief Summary

Remember, the goal of this game is to win, not that you're in 90% of all price moves. Open your positions when certain patterns occur and realize your profits when the target price is reached or at the first sign that the offer exceeds demand.

These basic principles apply to every time horizon, including day trading. If you are long-term oriented, use weekly charts. This will lead to many false signals, but there are indeed the stops. You will only earn money by studying countless charts and drawing your entry points, exit points, and stop loss. Thereby you internalize these approaches and make them suitable. After that, you could succeed in trading. One of the hardest things in trading is closing a position towards the end of an outbreak or during a buying spike. Just tell yourself that you are a nice person: everyone wants to have the stock, and you give yours.

The General Motors study might be one example of how you can create a supply-demand based trade system. Create two charts: one shows what you should have done and the other what you really did. Learn by comparison. Recognize the forces that act at important turning points.

Practical Application of the Elliott Wave Theory

The Elliott Wave Theory confuses many traders. In this chapter, we do not want to discuss the ambiguity of this theory, but we apply it to a trading plan that should develop into a successful approach. This theory is one of the best theories of the Cycle because it allows non-harmonic movements.

There are many different approaches to securities trading. These are roughly divided into fundamental and technical approaches. Some technicians like to mix both methods for an optimal market approach. The fundamental access includes bushels, hectares, consumption units, revenues, book values and so on. Technical Analysis examines past price movements and predicts future ones. In 1939, Elliott published a series of articles describing the principle of Elliott waves. The Elliott Wave Theory is one of the best technical methods for market analysis, and the serious-interested should certainly include it in his studies.

Is it possible to predict price trends using the Elliott Wave Theory and use this information profitably? The answer to that is a cautious yes if you do not make the theory an exact science. The Elliott Wave Theory allows harmonic and non-harmonic course movements. Most cycle theories use principles based on harmonic movements. As soon as nonharmonic movements occur, it becomes difficult.

The following summary of the Elliott Wave Theory reduces the ideas to a useful size:

1. Ascending moves consist of five waves, two of which are corrections. Falling movements are counterproductive. The odd waves run in the direction of the main motion. Straight waves run against the main direction. Shaft 2 corrects shaft 1. Shaft 5 corrects shaft 4. Sometimes there are nine or more waves. Elliott solves this problem by calling these movement extensions.

2. The endpoint of shaft 4 is higher than the height of shaft 1. Elliott specifies lengths proportions exactly, such as that the shaft 4 should be shorter than the waves 3 and 5. However, it has been found that this is not necessarily true.

The movements are divided into waves that are one degree smaller. What does "one degree smaller" mean? This question is difficult to answer, and that is one of the reasons why applying the theory is so difficult. One suggestion is to look for it in the next shorter timeframe. If you have a daily chart, look for the smaller grade on a 30-minute chart. The next smaller degree also needs five waves to complete the higher-order wave 1 and is therefore identical to the daily chart.

71

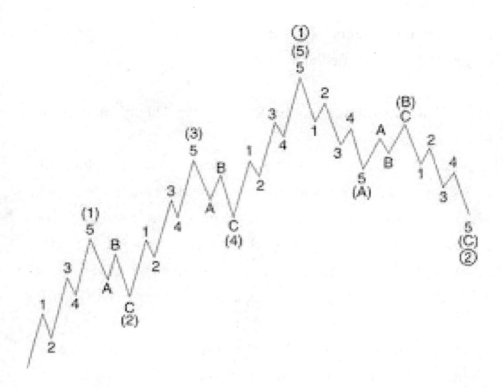

Triangular Corrections

Triangular corrections consist of a five-point pattern (ABCDE) after a thrust. The type and position of such a pattern often allow conclusions to be drawn as to whether a turnaround is pending or not.

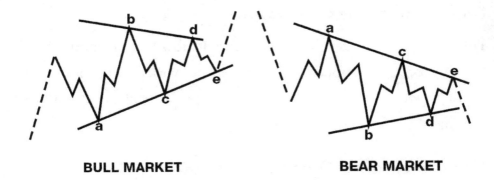

BULL MARKET   **BEAR MARKET**

A-Shaped Corrections

The length and duration of the first correction wave or A-shaped correction of the thrust are of utmost importance for determining the further course of the total correction and the probability of a turnaround.

Look for the application of the A-wave (the first correction wave to increase) to determine the type of correction and the probable direction of the price after the correction has been completed. Then, you can see four possible price movements. If the extent of the A correction wave is the same, the following should be deduced:

* 25% - 35%: Indicates a single correction wave.
* 35% - 50%: Indicates a three-wave correction.
* 50% - 75%: Indicates a five-wave correction.
* Over 75%: mostly a possible trend reversal.

73

Prediction of the Corrections

This type of price development can lead to a turnaround. Here are the forces of supply and demand at work. A reaction at a distance of 75% from the starting point makes a clearer statement than a low-25% reaction.

Understanding Options Terminology

For logical reasons, the option's duration is a factor. If you'll like an asset to be controlled for five years rather than one year, normally, having it controlled for a longer period of time would cost more. Alternately, it would not cost as much, in the event that you needed the asset controlled for just one day,

This is because the more the asset is being controlled, the more likely it is that something can happen (there's that word again) to affect its price. If for example, the property was controlled for just one day, it isn't too likely that a major real estate bargain involving your property will be reported that day.

Chapter 3 - Options Risk and Reward

Money management is only included in the trading plan by about one-tenth of all private traders. Just because a trader does not have a lot of capital does not mean that he cannot apply the principles of money management. Many traders are of the opinion that these ideas can only be used by large asset managers and institutions.

Money management also implies that the potential risk, taking into account the preferences of the trader, is set in relation to the expected profit. The goal is to set a desirable yield rate and then minimize the associated risk. Trading generally requires four decisions:

1. Buy/sell (system or strategy)?
2. Which security is traded?

3. How many contracts or shares of value are traded?

4. What is the share of capital risked on a trade?

The first decision is about the trading process itself without taking into account money management. The other three decisions involve maximizing profit and minimizing risk directly. The foundations of risk and reward should be considered from the start in the development of a trading system and must become an integral part of the system.

If a trader works profitably right from the start and has thus increased his trading capital, then he cannot be ruined by four losses (as long as his bet remains the same). Although the number of consecutive losses that would lead to ruin increases with time, so does the likelihood of multiple losses following one another. The following formula calculates the probability of ultimate ruin (WR) over time:

WR = (1-VT / 1 + VT) AH

VT stands for the trader's advantage (percentage winners - percent losers), and AH is the initial trading units. If the initial capital of a trader is $ 20,000 and his bet per trade is $ 5,000 then AH = 4. The following example calculates the probability of ultimate ruin:

Total Capital § 20,000	Total Capital $ 20,000	
Deployment $ 5,000	Deployment § 2,500	
Advantage of the Trade	10% Trades' Advantage	10%

Chance of Ruin	44.8%	Chance of Ruin	20.1%
Total Capital $ 20,000		Total Capital $ 20,000	
Bet $ 2,000		Bet $ 1,000	
Advantage of the Trade	10%	Advantage of the Trade	10%
Chance of Ruin	13.4%	Chance of Ruin	1.8%

These numbers apply only when you trade one contract at a time. With changing contract numbers, the risk of ruin changes dramatically. Moreover, these calculations assume that, in the case of a profit, the amount is always the same and corresponds to the loss in the negative case. As mentioned above, the risk of ruin is determined by the percentage of winners, the ratio between winners and losers, and the size of the bet. So far, we have disregarded the relationship between winners and losers. In real life, most successful trading systems score less than 50% winners and win-loss ratios above 1.2.

The risk of ruin is an interesting indicator, but it does not give much insight into how to use or manage capital efficiently. For self-preservation, it is best not to put everything on one card. If you choose your bets well and follow a system with a positive bias, the risk of ruin is very low.

The Capital Allocation Model

Now you know the tools you need to understand our capital allocation model. First, we'll show how capital is allocated to a one-market portfolio using a small selection of data. Later, we will apply the same approach to a two-market portfolio. At the end of the chapter, we will show the efficiency of the capital allocation model using a true system of small and medium accounts.

As you know, our goal is to maximize profit while minimizing risk. This goal must be achieved without exceeding the limits of justifiable risk. To reach the goal, we need to know how much capital is to be allocated to each market and what number of contracts should be traded. In this model, capital is calculated from the market value of the account, the average monthly returns, and the market risk. The market value is simply the starting capital with which we begin our trading. In these examples, the returns do not add up; we use the initial capital for all calculations. The average monthly income is the capital that we can expect to gain from our system. Market risk is the amount we can lose per day on a trade. Asset managers use a variety of metrics to assess market risk:

• Mean Range: The average of the ranges of the last three to 50 Days, which is converted into a monetary amount in US $. For example, if the average spread is 40 points for the Swiss franc over the past 10 days and the Swiss franc is $ 12.50, the market risk is $ 500. The likely amount of market movement is the average spread of the last x days. This does not always have to be

78

right, but the capital allocation model needs to be built on certain probabilities.

• The average change in closing prices: The average change in closing prices over the last three to 50 days says more about the risk, as this value indicates the expected risk if the position is held.

• Mean change in positive closing prices versus negative closing prices: the average change in the negative closing prices over a period suggests the risk of holding a long position.

• The standard deviation of closing prices: The standard deviation of the closing prices gives a more accurate picture of the risk, as the daily deviation is displayed with a probability of 68%. This calculation is a bit more complex, but it does not cause any problems with the computers available today.

In whatever way we measure the risk, it is the most important variable to watch and the most important component of the capital allocation model.

A Market Portfolio

Whether the system trades futures or stocks makes no difference. Before we can allocate capital, the average monthly income and market risk must be determined on the basis of a contract. We also need to determine how much of our capital we are willing to risk per trade. But we cannot know that yet, because that's exactly what we want to find out.

Cumulating Of Results

Cumulating means here the process of capital allocation based on the current portfolio or deposit value. The current portfolio value results from the start-up capital as well as the already completed positive and negative trades. When it comes to large sums of money, accumulation is very good: the capital invested increases or decreases depending on the current value of the deposit. If a trading plan is successful, then each trade will be given more capital; but if it is bad, then there is less capital available for each trade. Note that we have found that cumulating is very good when it comes to large sums. This limitation stems from the belief that the allocation should not be extended until the seed capital of smaller accounts has not been at least doubled or tripled. Even good systems can crash after a series of wins, and if a smaller account does not cumulate, there is still some capital left for bad times. If accumulation is of interest to you (and it should, if you have significant sums of money), then you can build it into the capital allocation model with a small change. In the formula, do not use seed capital as total capital (GK), but use the current value of the deposit.

Chapter 4: Analyzing Mood Swing in the Market

The Main Configurations of the Market

The high volatility of the markets shows how important it is for a trader to know how to rank the various market configurations. We can distinguish three main configurations (uptrend, downtrend, trading range). Before developing these configurations, we will explain the interest of the trader to master them.

There Are Three Main Types Of Markets:

- The uptrend market;

- The market in a downtrend;
- The market without trend (trading range).

Each type of market presents opportunities on which the trader can capitalize only by adopting an appropriate strategy:

In a bullish market, he will have to favor a mainly buying strategy; in a downtrend, it will have to adopt a sell strategy in a market without trend, the trader will have to favor the quick return and therefore a strategy of options trading or day trading by positioning itself to the purchase around the important supports and the sale around major resistances. Modern markets are so volatile that a simple buy-and-hold strategy no longer has a place even for the long term.

The Market Is Uptrend

A bullish market is characterized by a succession of lower and higher points, and higher and higher points. In a clear uptrend, the corrective phases (drop legs) are less important in amplitude than the impulsive phases (legs of rising). This property is very important because it provides a valuable indication of the possibility of a trend reversal. When a corrective leg has a greater amplitude than the impulsive leg (bullish in a bull market), then the uptrend is likely to be challenged. The trader will have to reconsider the current trend and avoid positioning himself for the purchase under these conditions.

A downtrend market is characterized by lower and higher points, but also by lower and lower points. In this type of market, rebounds often have less amplitude than bearish legs, the main characteristic of a bear market. In a trending market, the movements that go in the direction of the dominant trend are still the most powerful. As for the uptrend, the turnaround can be anticipated. This requires the recovery to be larger than the last bearish wave.

The Market without Trend

In a trendless market, there is no clear trend, and low points and high points are often confused. Buyers and sellers are testing themselves and no clear consensus is at work.

According to Wilder, markets evolve in trend one-third of the time and do not draw any clear trend during the remaining two-thirds. This property is important because investors are often victims of momentum bias. They tend to mechanically prolong the recent course evolution. If the course progresses during the last sessions, they are convinced of the continuation of its rise and many traders are trapped by positioning themselves around resistance or slightly above2. Conversely, in the case of a decline in stock prices, investors say that this decline will continue and are trapped by opening a position around major support.

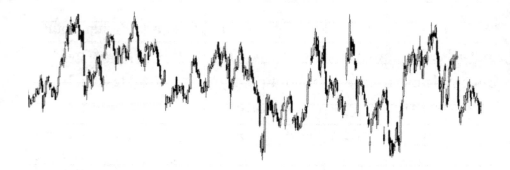

The good trader can wait patiently for the right moment before opening a position. Professional traders seek to position themselves at the beginning of an impulsive movement and avoid exposure by taking unnecessary risks when the market is not predictable. Good traders are people who can adapt to changing market conditions. As we will see later, markets fluctuate differently depending on whether we are in an uptrend, bearish trend or a trending market. In a bullish (bearish) market, the trader will be able to afford to buy (sell) up (down) and sell (buy) even higher (low), even if that is not ideal.

This is not the case in a market without a tendency where the trader will have to buy low and sell high, that is to say, sell the resistors and buy the supports and do not hesitate to go in and out quickly if the conditions require it. In a market without trend, many investors lose patience and position themselves impulsively, thus losing their capital and therefore the opportunity to participate in the real movement. They will often buy resistors and sell media. In trend markets, on the contrary, they will have the annoying habit of taking their profits hastily. These errors, consequences of psychological bias present in traders, must imperatively be corrected.

Trend Lines

Trend lines are often used by traders to identify bullish points in an uptrend and highs in a downtrend. In a bull market, the trend line goes through at least two low points. Conversely, in a downtrend market, the trend line will join at least two high points. It is possible to adjust trends over time based on new information: sharper, more marked trends may indeed appear as the trend initially traced becomes obsolete.

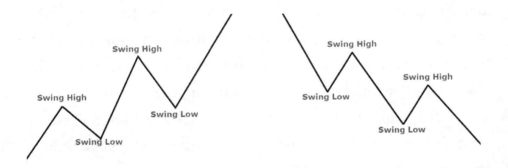

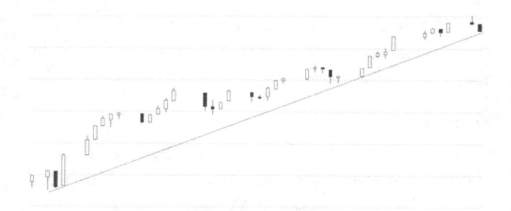

Conditions of Effectiveness of a Trend Line

The success of trend lines is justified by their effectiveness in identifying good levels of support and resistance. In other words, they sometimes make it possible to give with surprising precision these minor levels of reversal when a trend has already started. They also offer the possibility of identifying the state of the trend and anticipating reversals or simply corrective movements. In what follows, we try to give some elements to explain their effectiveness.

A first approach advances the argument of a stock market evolution respecting a "natural" phenomenon. There would exist on the market, and on all time horizons, trends that would respect a speed of progression and therefore a certain angle. The famous trader and analyst WD Gann explains that to last, a trend line must have a 45-degree angle. Not to mention natural phenomenon, we can say that a course of courses with a low slope indicates a slow movement that will probably abort. Conversely, when the slope is steep, the movement is too impulsive and will quickly run out of steam. The ideal is, therefore, to have an average slope (45 degrees), a sign of a healthy impulsive movement.

Another militant element in favor of trend lines is the fact that they are known to most operators. As we have seen, their validity will be strengthened because of the phenomenon of self-fulfilling prophecies. In concrete terms, a bullish trader will draw a trend line to identify the probable drop-off point for the stock, which will be a good buy with low risk. In the opposite case, it will draw a downtrend line to identify sales levels.

The importance of a trend line depends on the number of points it connects. The higher the number of rebounds on the right, the greater the importance. This is explained in particular by the mimicry of operators, which reinforces the strength of this line. In addition, the trend lines can be plotted over several time horizons (long, medium and short term), but the long-term trend lines or just to take them are those whose reliability is the most important. The trader will enjoy a return to the right of support (resistance) to strengthen its position buying (seller) and especially as the quality of the trend is proven.

Finally, a trend line, to be effective, should not be too steep. A parallel can be drawn with running: a sprinter will run out of steam quickly and will not be able to travel a long distance, while a runner will have the resources to travel the same distance. Similarly, if prices accelerate strongly, a consolidation is likely because it will allow the market to catch its breath before continuing its impetus.

We see on the PPR stock that the break in the trend line did not stop the market from continuing its upward movement. The stock just consolidated before heading back up. It is not uncommon for a rise to continue for a long time without being exhausted. Many traders will be trapped because they will seek to anticipate the turnaround. This is why the trader should always wait for the convergence of several signals before playing the corrective movement, and not be content with recent progress to justify his sell decision.

Finally, Elder recommends when drawing a trend line to avoid extremes because they are not representative. He prefers to use the support areas as levels to connect.

Finding a Trend Reversal Using a Trend Line

Rupture of a trend line is an important reversal signal. This signal is all the stronger as the trend line is significant (it has been used on many occasions to support the current trend). The break of a bullish or bearish straight line materializes the end of a market dynamic: the operators who should have strengthened their positions near the trend line proved to be weaker than the opposing side (the bearers), thus allowing the rupture of the right and all the dynamics of the market. The change in trend thus seems clear.

A broken bullish straight line immediately becomes a line of resistance against which the market will crash; this is very often shown by a pullback (return to the right of a trend that has just been broken). The market thus tests the strength of the support that has become resistance (or vice versa). Beware; the break of a trend line cannot alone constitute a signal of a reversal of the market, as shown by the example of the title PPR. It only alerts the trader about the possibility of consolidation.

Canals or Channels

A channel (Canal) is a figure directly related to the analysis of trend lines studied previously. The tracking is simple: once a bullish trend has been determined, it is a question of finding a parallel to the tendency to cover all the evolution of prices. Over the period when the trend is observed (straight line connecting the extreme points), we thus obtain a channel in which the courses evolve harmoniously.

The channel will tuck into a trend by allowing impulse turning points to be determined through trend lines, but also corrective turning points through the upper channel of the uptrend channel - or the bottom line for a downtrend channel.

The courses thus vary between these two lines: the first constitutes the support line of the canal, where the courts come to rest; the second represents the resistance line of the channel (or top of the channel) against which the market stumbles.

As for trends, it is possible to distinguish short, medium and long-term channels. The importance of a channel depends on its duration of evolution, but also on the number of times each line of the channel has been affected. To be considered a canal, you need at least two impacts on each side. The higher the number of impacts, the more important the channel is.

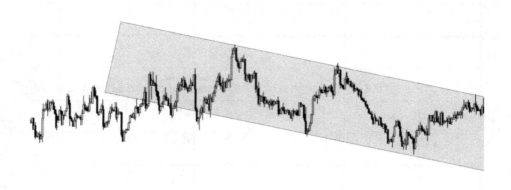

Intermediate Lines

In practice, prices do not move stubbornly between the lower bound and the upper bound. They sometimes have trouble passing intermediate areas within the canal. It is possible to draw parallel straight lines to the channel which constitute as many lines of support or minor resistance for the courses. However, the number of real intermediate rights is limited; one generally finds only one, even two. They are very often halfway through the channel and are real tests to know if the courses will reach the top or bottom. In the case of a bullish channel, the break in the intermediate resistance line often indicates that the market will reach the top of the channel.

It is also possible to distinguish within a channel small intermediate channels that allow, for example, the market to move from one terminal to another. Sometimes, too, a new channel emerges inside the canal, which appears more and more relevant, and which will eventually replace the old one that has become obsolete.

For the operator, the use of a channel is very simple: if it is a bullish channel, it will buy at the bottom of the channel to sell at the top, and eventually, become a seller. This rule will apply depending on the quality of the channel; for example, if the channel's resistance line seems fragile, it will not sell itself, it will simply take profits. We will also use the information given by the behavior of the courts facing the intermediate line. We will also use the information given by the small intermediate channels, or small lines of minor tendency.

Rupture of the Canal

Two kinds of breaks can be envisaged: either the trend is confirmed and reinforced (it is an upward outflow of the uptrend channel or the decline of a downtrend channel), or it is reversed, and it is then a possible change of trend (downward release of a bullish channel and exit up a downtrend channel). The break is all the stronger as it is done in a large volume.

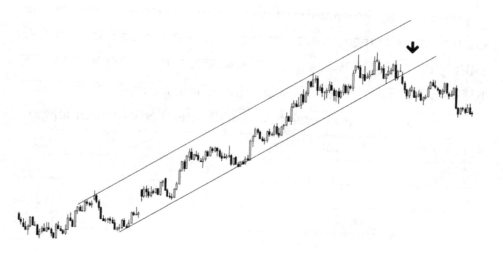

The operator has several elements to identify a possible rupture of the channel: in the case of a downward exit of a bullish channel, we usually notice that the courses have no strength, they do not arrive for example more to pass the intermediate right but stumble against it regularly. These elements are usually the first alarm signals.

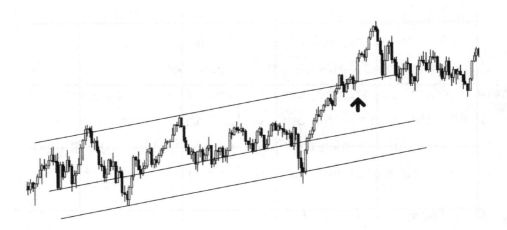

Precautions When Detecting a Signal

The breaking of a bullish channel does not necessarily mean a sell signal, just as the break of a bearish channel does not always correspond to a buy signal. This is a simple indication that will need to be supported by other elements to become a relevant signal.

The trader must convince himself that there is no absolute truth about the financial markets and that he must position himself only when the probabilities are favorable to him.

How to Detect the End of a Trend?

Can trend reversals be identified using chart analysis? We will see that it is possible to plot a reversal graphically, but for this, the trader will have to make sure that several criteria are respected: it is necessary to have a clear trend (for example, a trend line whose impulsive movements have a greater amplitude than corrective movements); the breaking of a major trend line or a major support is often a precursor signal of reversal; and finally, the various researches show that a figure of large turnaround (thus which took some time to be formed) will often be at the origin of an important corrective movement.

The Trend Reversal

After a downward movement (bullish), the title draws a bullish leg (bearish) whose amplitude is greater than the previous bearish (bullish) leg. This configuration signals a probable reversal of the trend and indicates the imminence of a bullish (bearish) departure or simply the cessation of the current trend and the entry of the market in a phase without a trend.

This presentation of trends has been deliberately simplified because, in fact, the range of movements is much richer.

Nevertheless, it is important to have a clear idea of the main trends in the markets before refining the analysis. The AGF stock is the typical case of a stock that draws a strong uptrend with very few corrections. It was difficult for a buyer to find a low point allowing him to position himself in the direction of the trend.

How Are Trends Formed?

Trends are a common phenomenon in the markets, but their training is often misunderstood by operators. Dow has developed a theory to provide relevant explanations for this phenomenon and can usefully be applied to current markets, regardless of the period used.

Chapter 5 - Sector Analysis: Technical and Fundamental

The Basic Principles of Technical Analysis

To better understand the technical analysis, we will summarize its fundamental principles; we will show the importance of the psychological dimension of technical analysis.

Fundamental Principles

Based on the work of renowned technical analyst John Murphy, we will present the main properties of technical analysis:

Technical analysis focuses on what is, rather than what should be. It is interested in the market itself and not the external factors that it reflects or that may have influenced it. It describes market movements, not the reasons behind them.

This method focuses on the psychology of the operators and not on the fundamentals. Indeed, what matters is not the news but the way operators react to it. This is a strategic approach to the stock market and not a fundamental approach, whose main purpose is the search for the intrinsic value of the asset. The technical analysis does not question the concept of fundamental value but argues that there may be lasting divergences between the stock price and the latter.

The market value is entirely and solely determined by the game of supply and demand. Supply and demand depend on many factors, some of which are rational and some not. The market results from the permanent interaction of all these behaviors and the differences of interpretation of the speakers. Fundamentals are just one price determinant among many others.

The courses evolve according to trends that can last a certain time. The trend changes are due to a change in the dominant consensus that will change the balance of power between suppliers and applicants. The graphs consider all the information available at a given moment. History repeats itself and markets are governed by the psychology of crowds. The phenomena of euphoria and panic are very often found on the markets and this cyclically. The following sentence, attributed to the famous speculator Jesse Livermore, sums up perfectly these words:

"I learned early on that there was nothing new on Wall Street. Indeed, speculation is as old as the hills. What is happening today in the markets has happened in the past and will happen again in the future."

These basic principles are favored by many leading operators (analysts, traders ...)

Consideration of the Psychological Dimension

Fundamental analysis focuses on the real value of a financial asset but neglected psychological component, determining for the proponents of the behavioral approach. This approach has shown that psychological biases explain price shifts in relation to the fundamental value. Technical analysis, therefore, takes into account this psychological dimension and focuses on the emotions of operators.

The fundamentals are supposed to be known to all, and the technical analyst's main task is to determine how the operators react to economic news. Basic information (growth rate, inflation rate, unemployment rate, contracts signed by a company, etc.) has a significant impact on stock prices, but most professional traders attach importance even greater at the behavioral reaction of traders.

Finally, as we have seen above, history repeats itself, and in financial markets governed by crowd psychology, it is common to note that the phenomena of euphoria are followed by panic movements.

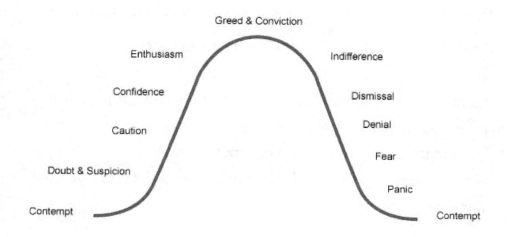

In a reference book, Gerald Loeb explains that a stock market price is only partly determined by a balance sheet and an income statement:

"It is much more by the hopes and fears of humanity, by greed, ambition, events beyond the reach of humanity such as natural disasters, inventions, stress and tensions in the financial world. Time, discoveries, fashion, and innumerable causes that it is impossible to enumerate."

The famous American financier Bernard Baruch going in the same direction as he explains:

"Fluctuations in the stock market do not correspond to the recording of events as such, but to human reactions to these events or how millions of men and women feel the potential impact of these events on the future. In other words, the stock market is a reflection of individuals."

Technical analysis also helps to take a strategic approach capitalizing on the emotions of other traders. The great economist Keynes was also a great speculator. In his financial operations, he relied heavily on crowd psychology and put aside basic analysis, which may seem surprising to a person who has had such a strong impact on economic theory. In fact, we owe him the following sentence: "There is nothing more irrational than investing rationally in the markets. This sentence does not mean that the investor must be irrational, but rather that the use of analytical tools considered rational must be used vigilantly. In his General Theory of Employment, Interest, and Money, published in 1936, John Maynard Keynes describes the markets as follows:

"Most professional investors and speculators are less concerned with making accurate forecasts in the long run than with predicting the future changes to the conventional valuation base shortly before the general public. In fact, the unacknowledged object of enlightened investment is to steal the departure, as Americans say so well, to be smarter than the public and to pass the wrong or belittled piece to the neighbor."

The Law of Supply And Demand

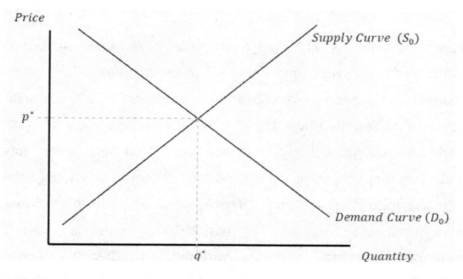

Technical analysis assumes that all the necessary information to the decision is contained in stock prices. The graphs represent a good barometer of investor psychology. Indeed, the technical analysis considers that it is the operators who are at the origin of the stock market fluctuations and not the economic and financial news. If a stock goes up it is that there are simply more buyers only sellers; conversely, if a stock is down, it means that the sellers are in surplus and plummet the stock prices. If this view of market fluctuations is also shared by fundamental analysis, the two methods diverge on the determinants of stock prices:

For the fundamental analysis, the officers and the plaintiffs focus essentially on the real value of the security. Security will be asked if it is undervalued (price below its fundamental value) and conversely it will be offered when the stock price is higher than its intrinsic value. Investors are rational and position themselves solely on the basis of the fundamental value of the security.

For technical analysis, the concept of fundamental value is not necessarily called into question. However, the security can fluctuate quite a bit before returning to its fundamental value. In addition, technical analysts consider it difficult to gather all the information needed to perform a fundamental analysis worthy of the name. It is for this reason that technical analysts seek, first of all, to identify the forces involved in order to determine the probable evolution of prices. The technical analysis simply seeks to answer the following question: "Which bull or bear will win the fight?"

The reality is that behind every offer or each application, there are many explanatory factors of fundamental and psychological. The theory of conventions explains that it may be rational to include in its analysis factors that have no connection with fundamentals, such as fashion phenomena for example. The stock price results from the permanent interaction of all these behaviors and the fundamentals11 are only one price determinant among all the others. The prices evolve according to "tendencies", which can last a certain time, because of the existence of a dominant convention. A change of trend can be explained in different ways: the fragility of the convention is updated by the financial community which turns away quickly from the financial asset (example of the technological values); the players have positioned themselves massively for the purchase and cannot, therefore, more support the market. Any bad news will have a massive effect and will cause massive sales related to the panic of operators.

Some technical analysts consider that there is no contradiction with the assumption of market efficiency since the graphs take into account all the information available at a given moment. Nevertheless, they forget that fundamental analysis considers operators to be rational, which is not the case for technical analysis. Market movements are predictable because the stakeholders regularly make the same mistakes and systematically deviate from this state of rationality.

Technical Analysis Is Not a Crystal Ball

Technical analysis is a method that can predict the evolution of prices with some reliability, even if it is not an exact science. This pragmatic method focuses primarily on the psychology of operators. It was developed by people operating on the financial markets (Charles Dow, GANN, Homma, Schabacker, and others). The technical analysis serves mainly as a market barometer and can detect excessive movements of crowds. Some of its detractors equate it with a crystal ball, whereas it is simply an effective tool for analyzing market movements.

There is no such thing as a martingale on the financial markets, that is, an infallible system that makes it possible to win every time. First of all, the only "martingale" is the result of hard work, iron discipline and the courage to stand up even when events are unfavorable.

Operators generally have imperfect knowledge of technical analysis. In addition, it should be noted that the mastery of this approach is insufficient to succeed in the markets. Indeed, it is not enough to correctly predict the evolution of stock prices to beat the markets. The trader must also develop certain qualities that have nothing to do with his analytical know-how (independence of mind, absence of ego, self-control, acceptance of uncertainty and risk).

The Reasons for the Current Success of Technical Analysis

Technical analysis is now more and more popular. We will list some explanatory elements of this current success.

The Limits of Fundamental Analysis

First of all, part of the success of technical analysis can be explained by the somewhat dull assessment of the fundamental analysis. This approach has been strongly criticized in recent years due not only to the bad - or even "misleading" -

recommendations of financial analysts but also because of the numerous financial scandals.

Laura Unger (president of the SEC13 in 2000), in a report, showed that 99% of the recommendations of the 28,000 US financial analysts were to "buy" or "keep" securities in March 2000. In addition, some stars of financial analysis did not stop their buying recommendations despite the market downturn. This has been very misinterpreted by individual investors and has given rise to numerous lawsuits.

Henry Blodget, an analyst at Merrill Lynch, waited until August of 2000 to lower his rating on e-Toys Inc. and Pets.com Inc. (which he recommended for buying when they had already lost more than 75% of their value.)

Mary Meeker, a senior analyst at Morgan Stanley, gained tremendous notoriety by issuing a very positive report on Internet values in 1995. After March 2000, she remained on the purchase and the titles she advised, including Priceline.com and Drugstore.com, literally collapsed.

Even after assuming that fundamental analysis has a predictive quality, the many financial scandals have shown that it is very difficult for an investor, whether individual or professional, to obtain complete and reliable information on the fundamental value of a security. Operated by insider operators taking advantage of their privileged position.

Chapter 6 - Designing a Trading Plan

Flexibility: Adapting Your Strategy to Market Conditions

The trader must never be obstinate, he must agree to adopt. This situation is obviously delicate. A good trader must rigorously apply his trading plan, while not considering the rules of the plan as immutable. Traders often apply the same strategy regardless of market configuration. The good trader considers the different market conditions and develops the most effective strategies for each situation. Thus, some day-traders have a strategy for opening, another for mid-day and finally one for closing. Others have adopted specific strategies for bull markets, bear markets and for trend-free markets. A good trader is able to adapt to changing markets and new conditions.

In addition, market conditions change over time (the market of the 2000s is different from that of the 1990s). Some effective strategies have not been effective today.

Nevertheless, the adaptation of the strategy must be based on in-depth research work and a critique of the methods used. The trader should never question his system when operating in real-time because it can be harmful. This phase of reflection should always be conducted calmly: the trader must prioritize strategic thinking before the fight and apply his strategy calmly in the heat of the moment.

Finally, for the great trader Mark Weinstein, "no approach in technical analysis works all the time. You have to know when to use each method. I do not believe in mathematical systems that approach markets in the same way. I use my person as the system and I constantly change the input to achieve the same output: profit."

The professional trader is constantly adapting its strategies to market conditions. He questions his system and tries to improve it with the aim of performance. Some principles are immutable, but it is still possible to improve certain rules or techniques of opening and closing positions, and this is what the big trader should be trying to do by being flexible and adapting himself to the evolution of the market

Look For the Line of Least Resistance

The strategy must always stick to market circumstances. The trader must know the direction of the flows because it is by marrying that he dominates them. In trading, you should never oppose the course of things and respect the famous saying "trout is your ally". We must leave the market to dictate the procedure to follow and not pretend to want to impose our certainty.

Thus, when a market is without trend, it is dangerous to apply a trend tracking strategy. In this case, the trader will only have to buy support and sell resistance. The trader must pierce the intentions of his opponents, the object of the analysis. He must decipher the intentions of professional traders, including detecting the right signals and eliminating false signals.

Lessons Learned

A successful trader lets his profits run and quickly cuts his losses. As a result, it maximizes profits and minimizes losses and achieves gains on average greater than losses.

In low-performing traders, the average loss is usually greater than the average gain: they quickly exit their winning positions and return to hope mode when the market invalidates their point of view instead of facing reality. Everything seems linked: the successful trader has a high payoff ratio and an honorable probability of success, which allows him to take more risks and thus to record a superior performance.

Example of a Trading System

Suppose that the trader relies on the following criteria to open a position:

- To position himself only in the presence of a double-bottomed graphic figure;
- Bullish divergence on the validated RSI, - MACD higher than its signal line.

The trader has tested his system over quite a long history and he finds that it has a probability of success of 60% and a payoff ratio of 2. It is a profitable system that can be used in the markets. Nevertheless, the probability of success, as well as the payoff ratio, is based on past data, which the trader will never know for sure if they will happen again. The only thing he can handle is a risk, which proves the importance of money management.

Vary The Size Of Its Positions?

Some traders use the same size regardless of the market configuration. They consider equiprobable events and believe that each configuration must, therefore, be assigned the same risk capital. This approach does not seem optimal for us and we think that it is necessary to vary the size of the position according to the opportunity that presents itself: to increase the size of its position when the opportunity seems excellent and its potential still important; reduce the size of the opportunity does not really give satisfaction, or even completely out of it.

It should be noted that novice traders do the opposite: at the outset, they allocate the same risk to all opportunities (good or bad); after a series of gains or losses, they increase the size of the position, whatever the opportunity, and take significant risks. They are suffering new losses that push them to engage more and more transactions, but also to increase the size of their positions, which can sometimes lead to ruin.

The performance relies heavily on the trader's ability to vary the size of his exposure based on opportunities. Likewise, it involves taking bigger risks and accepting higher drawdowns. Despite this, we remain convinced that good traders take much less risk than others and remain cautious in their decisions, even if they are not afraid to take positions. They consider that without risk-taking there are no possible gains.

This point of view was also defended by Thorp in his famous book Beat the dealer, which discusses the importance of increasing one's risk when probabilities are in our favor. Nevertheless, he also insists that conditions only favor 10% of the time and that it is during this period that we must maximize our chances of success. The payoff ratio must be favored over the probability of success.

Many traders place a lot of importance on the probability of success because it means that they are often more right than wrong. In fact, the payoff ratio has much more weight than the probability of success.

The payoff ratio is often low for traders because of the psychological bias highlighted by Kahneman and Tversky. In fact, individuals have a much greater aversion for losses than the satisfaction gained from the gains made: a loss is twice as painful as the satisfaction gained from a gain of the same amount. It is for this reason that people tend to take profits very quickly and not take their losses (so not to execute their stops) or even to ignore any information about them because they seem too painful.

Chapter 7 - Different Options Styles

Options Trading

Options' trading is an extremely well-known trading style for a wide range of investors. It tends to be utilized when investing in a range of financial instruments as well as options, for example, futures, foreign currencies, and stocks. It's basically a style that is somewhere close to the specific short-term style of day trading and the longer-term approach of utilizing a buy and hold strategy.

It's typically a style utilized by those generally new to options trading, but at the same time, it's frequently supported by those who have higher experience also. There are various advantages to options trading and specifically, utilizing this style for trading options. Similarly, as with investment, there's a great deal of information, you ought to learn before really beginning.

What Does Options Trading Involve?

Options' trading is tied with searching for short-term price momentum and attempting to profit from that price force by buying and selling suitably. As the value of options contracts is to a great extent dependent on the value of basic securities, you are basically hoping to recognize the price energy of any financial instrument, for example, stocks, and afterward trade the significant options contracts as indicated by how you anticipate that the hidden security will move.

By and large, you will enter a position and after that exiting it a short period of time later. That period of time can be anyplace between several days or half a month, contingent upon to what extent you are anticipating that the price momentum should last.

With this style, you aren't as worried about the basic value of the securities involved and how they will perform in the long term as you would utilize a buy and hold investment strategy. While some basic analysis of the securities can surely be valuable, you are basically hoping to distinguish circumstances where a specific security is probably going to move sensibly altogether in price over a generally short period of time. This depends on trends and patterns. When you have recognized that circumstance, then you would then be able to buy or sell in like manner with a view to profiting from the price movements.

Options' trading is achievable utilizing most sorts of options, and you can utilize diverse orders to take short positions or long positions on distinctive contracts. You can even utilize a mix of various contracts and orders to make spreads which can significantly expand the number of chances for profiting. Spreads can likewise be utilized to limit risk presentation on a specific position by limiting potential losses.

There are really two distinct types of options trading options: discretionary and mechanical. Discretionary options trading depends on using your own analysis and judgment to make a decision. Mechanical options trading entails following a fixed regulation to determine fixed entry and exit spots, and you can even utilize software to determine what transactions you ought to make and when.

Why Use an Options trading Style?

Of the two most broadly known and acknowledged trading styles, options trading and utilizing a buy to hold investment strategy, options trading is the best style for options. The buy to hold strategy isn't generally appropriate by any means since options are basically short-term trading instruments. Most contracts end following a couple of months or shorter, and even the longer-term LEAPS become invalid at the end of a year. Thusly, options are the ideal instrument for options trading.

Options' trading is much less serious than day trading and furthermore significantly less time-devouring. With day trading, you must be ready to spend the entire day checking the markets while trusting that the opportune time will enter and exit positions. The levels of attention required can be exceptionally depleting, and it requires an unmistakable range of abilities to fruitfully utilize this style. Options trading, then again, is an ideal center ground for those that need to see a sensibly fast return on their money yet don't have room schedule-wise to devote to buying and selling throughout the day, consistently.

It's an incredible style for those that are relative amateurs and those that have full-time occupations or have other time responsibilities amid the working day. It's feasible to emphasize potential swings, enter the important position, and after that simply check how your position is faring toward the finish of every day, or even every couple of days, before choosing whether or not to exit that position.

You can end losses or utilize spreads, so you are never in peril of losing more money than you are okay with. You can really utilize spreads by different strategies, some of which are especially valuable for options trading when you aren't for all time checking price changes in the market.

The fundamentals of this style are moderately simple to understand, which another valid justification for giving it a go is. You don't need to have an immense measure of knowledge to begin; you simply need to know how options function and be ready to devote a sensible measure of time to search for the correct chances. Some risks are definitely involved. However, this style to a great extent, allows you to take absolutely any level of risk that you are alright with and allows you to make some fair profits.

Guidance for Options Trading

Investigating and planning is essential for anybody hoping to utilize this style. You should be very ready and have a smart thought of precisely what sorts of examples and patterns you are searching for and what kind of transactions you will make in some random circumstance. You definitely want a level of flexibility in the manner in which you trade, though it can have an unmistakable arrangement of targets and a characterized plan for how you will accomplish those objectives. The market is unstable, and it will require you to make changes in like manner. A strong plan, however, gives you a platform to work from.

Great investigative abilities are exceptionally helpful. You don't need to settle on choices as fast as though you were day trading, so you have time to break down circumstances and work out the best entry and exit spots purposes of a specific trend or pattern that you recognize. It's likewise critical to be quiet. If it happens that you can't find a decent entry point to exploit a price swing, at that point you need the discipline and persistence to hold up until the point that an open door presents itself. It's not necessary to make trades each day if there are no appropriate ones to be made, and the way to progress is actually about picking the correct chances and carrying out your transactions at the perfect time.

It's a smart thought to set the greatest losses on any position that you enter. It's improbable that you will get your expectations and conjectures right every time you enter a position, and sometimes the prices will move against you. You should, at all times be prepared to cut your losses and escape an awful position; it can and will occur, and you simply need to ensure that your great trades exceed your terrible trades.

So also, you ought to dependably have an objective profit for a position, and close your position when you have achieved that profit. Endeavoring to press additional profit out of an open position can simply bring about losing your profits. Your parameters for limiting losses can simply be set and locking in profits by options spreads, stop orders or a blend of both.

Options Brokers for Trading Options

A standout amongst the most imperative choices you have to decide on before beginning with this, or some other style, is which stockbroker would it be advisable for you to utilize? Utilizing an online broker isn't as important for options' trading as it is considered for day trading, yet you could utilize a conventional broker in the event that you needed. Notwithstanding, there are as yet numerous advantages to utilizing an online broker; for instance, they usually sell less expensive fees and commissions which will enable you to submit your requests.

- Position: Trading
- Trading Intensity: Low
- Holding Period: 1 to a half-year
- Time Commitment: Low
- Risk Level: Low

Not like other options trading styles, position trading isn't usually utilized for most financial instruments. Actually, it is practically one of a kind to trading subsidiaries, for example, futures and options. It is a generally safe style that is utilized to make a profit by exploiting a portion of the sure window that options can present. It isn't a style that ought to be embraced by novices, as it requires a complete comprehension of options and all the related elements.

Position trading is a style that is only utilized by professional and institutional traders. Market makers, for instance, would utilize this style to satisfy their job. However, it is truly not a style of that any easy-going or home trader ought to consider. Options trading is typically the best decision for many, or day trading for those that can make a full-time responsibility. It is still necessary to see how this style operates, however.

What Is Position Trading?

Position trading is a technique that is generally utilized by professionals that stand for banks and other big financial institutions. It's principally utilized for transacting derivatives and, specifically, options contracts. If this style is to be used, a trader has to know significantly something beyond how options function; really deep information of all the important qualities and elements that influence options and their prices is required.

Furthermore, it is necessary to have an entire comprehension of all the diverse strategies that can be utilized, how they operate, their advantages and disadvantages, and how they can be used relying upon winning market conditions.

The basic aim of this style is that as much as possible, the risk should be reduced, regardless of whether it implies making a low percentage of profits. Position traders often want to profit from directional moves in the market like the majority of the investors. However, their exercises are generally founded on supporting existing portfolios against those directional moves and endeavoring to make a profit from the time decay of options contracts.

Holding positions for really long periods of time is usually required, with the end goal to amplify the potential profit, and options are regularly held straight up until lapse. In spite of the fact that position traders may just hold positions for short periods sometimes, contingent upon the strategies being utilized and the market conditions, the fundamental meaning of a position trader is somebody who holds a position as long as possible.

Profiting From Position Trading

We have just clarified how this style is not generally appropriate for the occasional investor on account of the extraordinarily deep knowledge that is required. It ought not totally to be disregarded even if you truly feel you have understood all about options, however generally you will constantly be in an ideal situation utilizing an alternate style. Another explicit purpose behind this is the manner in which that position traders make their profit.

The general purpose of this style is to dependably reduce risk to the barest minimum. The level of risk is indicated by the profit levels to be made like most types of investing. While the facts confirm that the professionals can make a huge amount of money, this is on the grounds that they are managing large measures of capital.

The vast majority of the strategies utilized are based on endeavoring to ensure a specific sum of profit, anyway little that profit is. Maintaining reduced risk is considerably more essential than attempting to make the most profits. When trading with a big measure of capital, achieving returns of minuscule percentages can be particularly beneficial. Notwithstanding, for those that have a littler beginning capital, making any sort of huge money utilizing this style is extremely hard in fact.

Positions trading options aren't probably going to be the best style for many of options traders. It's basically the space of professional and institutional traders for two basic reasons. To start with, it requires a deep knowledge of everything identified with options trading, every one of the elements included, and all the achievable strategies that can be utilized. Second, it's just actually feasible to make any sort of huge profits with substantial beginning capital.

Market Makers

Market makers assume a critical job in options trading, and in certainty, they exist in the markets for a wide range of various financial instruments. They are basically there to keep the financial markets running productively by guaranteeing a specific level of liquidity. They are not your normal trader; they are professionals that have legally binding associations with the significant exchanges and complete a substantial volume of transactions.

It isn't important, that you comprehend what market makers do, except if you have goals to join a financial institution and secure occupation as one. Be that as it may, having an idea of why they exist, and the impact they have is in any case valuable.

The Role of Market Makers

The fundamental job of market makers in the options exchanges is to make sure that the markets run easily by empowering traders to buy and sell options regardless of whether there are no open orders to suit the required trade. They do this by keeping up the substantial and various arrangement of an extensive variety of various options contracts.

For instance, if a trader needed to buy certain options contracts yet there was nobody else at that time selling those contracts, at that point a market creator would sell the options from their very own portfolio or hold, to encourage the transaction. Moreover, if a trader needed to sell certain contracts yet there was no open buyer, after that, a market creator could execute the transaction by buying those contracts and adding them to their portfolio.

Market makers ordinarily ensure that there is both profundity and liquidity in the options exchanges. In the absence of the two, there would be altogether fewer transactions done, and it would be a lot harder to buy and sell options. There would likewise be fewer options in the method for various contracts accessible in the market.

Allowing traders to execute transactions immediately, regardless of whether there is no ready buyer or seller, thusly, guarantees that the exchanges work effectively and traders can generally buy and sell the options they desire to.

How Do Market Makers Operate?

As said earlier, market makers keep their very own portfolios that comprise countless options contracts. They trade in substantial volumes and can buy options from traders who want to sell and sell them to traders willing to buy. Without the producers, the market could easily cease, and options trading would turn out to be greatly hard.

In return for the imperative job they play in options trading, they have significant right inside the marketplace that allows them to basically make some type of profit on every single transaction they make because of the manner in which options are priced.

There are two primary perspectives to the price of options that any options trader ought to get. To begin with, the real price comprises two major segments: extrinsic value and intrinsic value. Besides, and this is applicable to how market makers work, they are priced on the exchanges with an asking price and a bid price. Anybody hoping to buy options contracts would pay the asking price from those contracts, while anybody composing or selling contracts would get the bid price.

The bid price is lower than the asking price; this means that any person buying contracts would pay a higher price than the person selling them would get. The difference between these two prices is referred to as the spread, and it's from this spread the market makers gain from. They are essentially allowed to sell at the asking price and buy at the bid price, consequently profiting from the spread.

Let's assume a case of specific options contracts that are trading with an asking price of $2.20 and a bid price of $2. Should a person place a request to buy these contracts, in the meantime as another person submits a request to sell these contracts, the market creator essentially goes about as an intermediary. They buy from the dealer, paying the bid price of $2.00, and afterward sold to the buyer at the asking price of $2.20, consequently making a $.20 profit for each contract traded.

Obviously, it won't generally be workable for a market creator to buy and sell contracts at the same time – generally, there would be little requirement for them in any case. This means that they are still strongly presented to the risk of price movements and time decay of the options they claim. The essential point of a market producer is to trade whatever a number of contracts as could be expected under the circumstances to profit by the spread, however, should likewise utilize viable positioning strategies to guarantee that they are not presented to a lot of risks.

In spite of the natural advantage of being a market producer proffered by the spread, it's still very feasible for them to lose money.

Who Then Are The Market Makers?

Market makers are typically people that work for banks, brokerage firms, and other financial institutions that are specifically contracted with an exchange or exchanges, to satisfy the job. As they are not permitted to trade in the interest of open investors and traders, they will utilize their very own capital to fund every one of their transactions.

They must show great prowess at what they do, with great expository capacities and a considerable measure of mental quality. At the point when the significant firms enroll market makers, they would more often than not be searching for a great deal of appropriate involvement and an unmistakable sign of the required range of abilities.

Chapter 8 - ETF's, Options and Other Tricks

Best Brokers for Options Trading

E-Trade's OptionsHouse platform and mobile application are the highest quality levels of option trading platforms. OptionsHouse at present gives traders premium-quality tools without the top-notch price tag. Best options trading platform.

Fidelity platform shows traders the correct way and gives them every resource they require as the trading goes. Options trading can be scary and confounding for new traders. Fidelity offers a monstrous measure of free research and information introduced in a way that is not overpowering for inexperienced traders. Best research and training.

Tastyworks has become famous in options trading. The brokerage, driven by its parent financial media organization, Tastytrade, offers probably the best rates in options trading matched with incredible tools and options for traders. The brokerage flaunts a low commission structure, finish with zero closing trade fees, depending on the kind of opening contract:

options on futures, futures, options on stocks, and stocks. Best lost cost broker.

EOption gives a proficient, nitty-gritty platform for active investors who prefer low expenses to an extravagant platform. The investment funds can be critical for cutting-edge stock and options traders who have different sources for the research and information they require.

Honorable mentions: Lightspeed, Merrill Edge, Options House, and Trade King

Do Not Believe Everything You Hear

One last admonition about picking a broker: Just because a sales representative or promotional material says a brokerage firm offers some new feature on their software or an exceptional service doesn't imply that it's quite true. As we know, some marketers are emissaries of frivolity, preferring to promote the positive and disregard the negative. In this manner, the cases you read in writing delivered by the firms themselves might be painfully exaggerated.

In all truth, managers and programmers frequently tell advertisement marketing specialists that some new service or product highlight will be available when the promotion turns out, and then fail to meet their own schedule. What's more, sales representatives are every now and then told things that are non-existent work better than they do—and, not being experts and ready to decide for themselves, just pass the misrepresentations along.

Our point is: Try to do more other than converse with the brokerage agent. Look at some reviews; online and in popular financial magazines here and there. Then speak with people who have to be in the industry long before you.

Secure Yourself with a Backup Plan

Be absolutely mindful, nonetheless, that regardless of how good a brokerage firm is painted as being, you'll more likely have an issue or two preceding all said and done. These could be the consequence of disturbances at the exchanges, with your broker's database, or with your own computer, Internet connection, or telephone line.

Or, you could even commit an exorbitant error as the consequence of stupid calculation errors. Approximately fourteen years back, we signed onto our internet browser to check the news and opening market indices —and nearly hopped into frenzy mode when the EarthLink™ start page showed the Dow down 397.85 for just 10 minutes after the opening. Obviously, it was simply a terrible calculation; the Dow was extremely down simply 7.85—however, the browser's numbers weren't right throughout the day. Had we followed up on those numbers, it could have been a catastrophe. Be that as it may, that is only the manner in which it is in today's powered-up world, kept running by PCs, encouraged by telephone lines and absolutely subject to the ideal execution of electrical transmission lines.

To shield yourself from the impacts of these mechanical caprices, build up a reinforcement plan that goes past simply hoping to get the telephone and call your broker when the framework goes down. This plan ought to include:

•	Be certain you generally have limits and stops set up on your weak positions—both profitable and unprofitable.

•	Be certain you completely comprehend the risks before attempting new strategies or starting new plays.

•	Printing out day by day printed copies of your open positions in the event that the broker's server fails.

•	Closely observing your account status, particularly your equity balance, and printing hard copies of key account outlines at any rate week by week.

With those protections set up, technical issues may cost you a little loss. However, you'll never confront overwhelming financial difficulty. What's more, should the broker encounter a total framework disappointment, your paper duplicates will kill any plausibility of debate in regards to your positions and value of accounts.

Concerns such as those highlighted earlier are legitimate. However, they're not really motivations to shy away from options trading—particularly given the technological and innovative advancements.

Chapter 9 - Options Strategies

How to Trade In Stocks

The Advantages of the Options Trading System

By opening a part of the position (half for example), we avoid losing a lot of money if we make a mistake on the meaning of the market. In a way, the trader tests the market. We only strengthen our position when the market gives us the reason. In this case, we expect confirmation or a new low point (in a bull market) or high point (in a bear market) in the current trend. For example, if we are buyers it is possible to strengthen one's position when the RSI lands on the neutrality zone. The placement of the stop will be slightly below the base which has been broken to strengthen the position.

This technique allows the trader to avoid the classic mistake of getting out of a winning position too early and hesitating to cut a losing position. If the position results in a loss, it will not be too big and therefore the trader will not hesitate to cut it. Indeed, when the loss is heavy, it is often painful and traders prefer to go into hope mode rather than face it. In addition, this approach allows the trader to play the movement in all its amplitude since it will strengthen its position which will prevent it from going out quickly.

In addition, the trader who strictly applies his plan will avoid downward averaging. This serious fault is often fatal. From now on, with this method, the trader will strengthen his position only when the market evolves in his direction and will not cut it too fast or with a small gain. Finally, the last advantage of this method is that it allows testing the market. If the stock does not react as expected, the loss will be only 50% of the loss that would have been incurred if the entire position had been opened at the very beginning. Thus, this method allows the trader to strictly adhere to the stock market adage: "Cut your losses and ride your winners."

The Limits of the Options Trading System

This method presents the risk of strengthening a position while a market reversal is emerging. It is not effective in a market without trend because the trader will strengthen its position on an extreme level (high point or low point). He must, therefore, be convinced that there is a tendency to apply this approach. This method adapts badly to a market without trend but even in this case, it presents limited risks.

The Classic System: Open Its Position in One Time

The classic method is to fully open its position and then take profits during the upward movement (for a purchase) or downward movement (for a sale).

The Limits of the Classical System

This system is mainly adapted to a market without a trend. It should be noted that the losses are much greater than for the options trading system and that the performance is not necessarily greater. Nevertheless, when the market is volatile this system is the most efficient. The trader will have to focus on carefully selecting his positions (thus increasing his probability of success) and taking profits faster.

A Pragmatic Method to Maximize Trading

One of the main attractions of technical analysis is that it does not present huge barriers to entry. It is less demanding than the fundamental analysis in terms of knowledge to acquire. Fundamental analysis generally requires long and solid academic training in economic and financial analysis. This training is usually difficult to acquire, which can discourage more than one.

The researcher Olivier Godechot conducted a sociological study on traders operating in a Paris trading room. This research found that traders and other financial operators had little control over economic reasoning. The author even goes ahead to say that the market economist was merely popularizing the economy and did not push his analyzes very far.

Moreover, even with this method of analysis, investors are not necessarily well equipped to understand the significant and persistent discrepancies in the price of a financial asset compared to its fundamental value. The tests conducted by Meese and Rogoff (1983) have shown that it is impossible for fundamental analysis to predict the evolution of exchange rates. They even go so far as to argue that a naïve model was often more efficient than a model based on fundamental analysis.

The frequent and large discrepancies between the price of a financial asset and its fundamental value (assessed by financial analysts) are hardly explained by the fundamentals or they are posterior. Finally, the technical analysis is not reduced in the short term as many experts say. This method offers reliability in the forecasts made, and this as well in the short term as on the medium and long term, as we will see it thereafter.

Equal Treatment for All Stakeholders

For the Orthodox school, an efficient market is characterized by the transparency of information. But many insiders (employees of a company, business bankers, family, friends, financial analysts, etc.) have some privileged information, which they can take advantage of. Everyone is not equal in the phase of information.

For the proponents of technical analysis, all the information available at a given moment is integrated into the courses. If a company intends to report poor results, it is likely that this information is visible on the price, and the technical analysis offers the opportunity to anticipate this negative news. Very often, insiders will seek to get rid of their securities, which cause a decline in stock prices (no apparent news) and are a sure sign for seasoned operators.

The role of the technical analyst is to detect the moments when a title will shift without valid reason and therefore to be alert all the time. The graph contains all the information investors' need, which puts them on an equal footing. Some economists even go so far as to say that technical analysis does not necessarily contradict the assumption of market efficiency since it is based on the same assumptions. This approach is attractive and reassures private investors, who have the same information as professionals.

With technical analysis, performance will be primarily a function of personal discipline and experience. Indeed, having the same information does not mean that its use will be the same for everyone. Some people will know how to exploit it better than others and will react appropriately. Implicitly, this means that using the same analysis tool does not necessarily imply consistency in decision making. The psychological dimension that explains the effectiveness of technical analysis also makes it possible to understand why individuals do not make the same decisions while basing themselves on the same information.

Technical Analysis Is Better Accepted By the Academic World

Considered originally as a naive model by the academic world, technical analysis is increasingly accepted today. Indeed, the assumption of the efficiency of the markets, dominant yesterday, is more and more questioned. The work done by behaviorists and conventionalists supports the idea that prices can strongly and durably shift their fundamental value for no good reason.

A. Orlean defends the idea of self-referential rationality, at the origin of rational speculative bubbles that can be formed even in the presence of perfectly rational individuals. Stakeholders will rationally use the dominant convention to make their decisions because they believe that it is better to follow the market than to refer to fundamental value.

Better yet, the work of the behaviorists gives an almost scientific character to the technical analysis. H. Krow likened technical analysis to behavioral analysis. In the preface of his book, he highlights three main schools of thought: fundamental analysis, random walk and finally the behavioral approach. According to Krow, technical analysis is the counterpart of behavioral analysis.

Closer to home, an article in The Economist in 1993 establishes a link between behavioral finance and technical analysis. This is only fair because technical analysis has focused on the behavior of individuals well before the emergence of the behaviorist approach. This pragmatic approach had, moreover, highlighted the existence of recurrent errors, the peculiarity of human nature. Thus, the famous: "Let your profits run and cut your losses quickly" is symptomatic of market reality. Indeed, stakeholders would tend to cut their winning positions too quickly and hesitated for a long time before closing their losing positions. This stock market adage, which cannot be dated precisely, has been demonstrated by the experiments of Kahneman and Tversky.

An Approach Acclaimed By Major Traders

A method is judged by its success. In a pragmatic way, the success of technical analysis can be explained simply by the spectacular performance of some of its users.

The problem of technical analysis is that it can be of formidable efficiency in the hands of a great trader, and represent an extreme danger for a novice trader. O. Godechot quotes in his work a trader who explains the reason for the success of the technical analysis in his trading room:

"The chief economist of the trading room makes many mistakes or justifies an economic event posterior while the chartist of the room is right in nearly 70% of cases."

On many traders surveyed by high-flying J. Schwager, over 80% said they only use technical analysis or in addition to fundamental analysis. Ed Seykota is a perfect example: a graduate engineer from MIT, this trader has achieved a performance of 25,000% over a period of sixteen years. He does not hesitate to say that he does not touch fundamentals - which he even calls "funnymentals" - and only uses models that use technical analysis.

According to him, "a good surfer does not have to master fluid physics and resonance to get a good wave. The goal is to feel when the wave will take shape and have the courage to seize it at the right time". The famous trader Bruce Kovner goes in this direction when he explains the effectiveness of this method:

"I use a lot of technical analysis and it's a fabulous method. It helps to clarify the fundamental analysis. Technical analysis is like a barometer. Fundamentalists who say that graphs are useless are like the doctor who feels it's pointless to take the temperature of his patient. That does not make sense. If you are a serious trader, you need to know where the market is, whether euphoria is dominant or whether pessimism prevails. The trader must know everything about the markets if he wants to have an advantage."

The approach of Kovner is rich in information. Indeed, according to this manager, technical analysis should not be considered as an exact science, but rather as a market barometer. It allows to know the forces involved and to guess the dominant feeling of the market. It is, as for the doctor, to take the temperature of the market, to make a diagnosis before recommending a remedy. However, Kovner being an exceptional trader, it is difficult to generalize his approach. It is true that operators often use technical analysis without real control and rarely operate as strategists.

These non-standard traders are an excellent ad for technical analysis. This method, which may seem esoteric and unscientific, draws its credibility and quasi-scientific character from the success of "some" of its users. What better argument for market efficiency than a person who has regular earnings over a long period of time and consistently uses the same method of analysis?

Nevertheless, these remarks must be nuanced. The success of these traders is not only explained by the method of analysis. Strong market experience, iron discipline, and personal talent have probably played a significant role in their success. It is important to note that many traders have been ruined several times before accumulating considerable fortunes, and that experience plays a fundamental role in the success of a trader.

Finally, the signals used in technical analysis evolve over time. If the phenomena of euphoria and greed are recurrent, the way in which they emerge can evolve. A good trader must, therefore, have the ability to adapt to changing markets.

Chapter 10 - To Do and Not to Do

The Strategist Trader

According to the strategic approach, price is the product of individual beliefs. For a strategist, only the beliefs of others count, even if they are unfounded. Yamina Tadjeddine took into account two scenarios: the other entire actors act as strategists and they will try to anticipate what others will do. André Orléan speaks of self-preferentiality to characterize this phenomenon: the trader will be determined by the beliefs of other stakeholders because the absence of a referent collectively admitted to base the price forces him to do so. It seeks to reduce uncertainty, and to do so it will mimic others ... only one operator is a strategist and all the others are naive stakeholders or rely on an untrained model to make their decisions.

This situation gives rise to two possibilities:
- The strategist cannot influence the prices and, in this case, the price corresponds to the fundamental value;
- The strategist has substantial financial means and enjoys a significant credit with the financial community. It has enough capacity to influence prices and will use it to maximize profit.

De Long, Shleifer, and Waldmann have shown by their model, in 1990, the rational investor will be determined based on ignorant or irrational investors. It will be prompted to handle the work of ignorant investor's passive investors in a destabilizing direction in order to increase their profits. If the myopic investors are trend followers, they buy when the prices go up and sell when the price drops. The interest of the rational investor will be to raise prices, to provoke a purchase by ignorant investors, and then sell on top to take advantage of the market downturn.

The best attitude is that of the strategist because the short-term movements are hardly explained by the fundamentals. Depending on the situation, the strategist will have to adapt his answer. In some cases, it may influence stock prices and use this capacity for its own benefit. In others, it will not have the financial power to do so, but may still adopt a strategic attitude without really influencing the markets. The fundamental value is not fixed and evolves according to different parameters. Take the case of a company with a potential deemed satisfactory by most financial analysts. It goes without saying that a simple political decision or a major technological innovation is enough to upset the game and therefore the fundamental value. What is good at one time is therefore no longer necessarily good at another, and we understand the interest of the investor to adopt a strategic attitude that is not limited to the fundamental value and takes into account the behavior other operators.

The optimal strategy for a trader is, therefore, to make the most profit on an action. The professional trader will prefer to sell undervalued security if he considers that the downside potential is not exhausted then will position himself to buy on a low point to play the movement of recovery: this investor will not be satisfied with part of the movement but will prefer to play the movement in all its amplitude.

To summarize, the trader whether institutional or particular must integrate that:
- Institutional traders master the art of strategy and have more resources than a trader. The risk of shifting the markets and suffer many constraints (legal, liquidity, etc.). On the other hand, they have reliable sources of information, advantageous brokerage fees, which gives them an undeniable advantage on the markets- the private trader is often in a weak position compared to the institutional ones: he can easily be manipulated but can hardly handle the big traders. On the other hand, there are niches from which it will be able to profit because its main advantage (compared to the institutional ones) remains the flexibility: a particular trader fixes his pro-rules and evolves freely on the markets. It does not really have constraints in terms of rules, markets worked, size of positions, liquidity, etc.

The Importance of Strategy

There is no perfect and ideal technique in trading that applies to all traders and all situations. We can even say that there are as many trading styles as there are traders. The market operator must be wary of the one-size-fits-all solution or miracle system simply because the markets are changing, and what works today will be less effective tomorrow. He must not try to be right, but to maximize his chances of success.

After defining the strategy, we will highlight the main strategies adopted in the business world and we will see to what extent they can be applied to trading.

Strategy Definition

A trading strategy can be defined as the art of detecting the best opportunities offered by the market and allocating the necessary resources to profit from it. It will consist of understanding the psychology of the speakers and developing a method to capitalize on this knowledge. The goal of the strategy is to be original, powerful and offer a real advantage over the competition.

The development of the strategy and its implementation imply for a trader to have a strong trading system and control his emotions. In fact, we realize that the trader is often the victim of his own bias, that he does not have a real system and that even if it is the case, it will systematically deviate.

The strategy is materialized by the strict and rigorous application of a trading plan including tested and tested rules that will allow the trader to capitalize on recurring figures without neglecting the risk. This strategy will make it possible to define:

How it will determine the entry points by taking into account the money management aspect as well as the technical aspect; the different techniques to make profits; the manner in which the stops will be fixed; the contingency plan which specifies the different approaches of the trader in the face of the disaster scenarios.

Strategy and tactics are often confused: the strategy aims at absolute performance, in other words, victory, whereas tactics are a means to achieve it. Strategy plays an important role as it allows the trader to get out of the chaos that reigns in the fight by keeping in mind firmly rooted principles.

Tactics are at the service of strategy and must never take too much liberty with respect to strategy. This principle is the key to victory, but it is often forgotten by traders and explains for a large part the failure of many of them.

The trading plan will, therefore, include different tactics but must also specify the global strategy of the trader that can be called vision. That is to say that the trader must in his trading plan specify how he sees himself in a few years (the vision) and indicate the strategy that will be put in place to achieve it

The Different Strategies

Several types of strategies make it possible to succeed. The strategy of global dominance by the costs mainly benefits institutional traders who have extremely low transaction costs and can benefit from small market movements. Generally, they work for large institutions and have a real advantage over individuals. Their fixed costs (hardware, software, offices, etc.) are reduced because of their size and the large sums they brew. In addition, they have an important information network that gives them a real advantage over others.

The Differentiation Strategy

For a company, differentiation is about creating a product that offers qualities that justify a higher price and a real advantage over the competition. This is the case of innovative products, quality of service, a more efficient organization of work, etc.

Similarly, the trader has every interest in differentiating himself from his competitors by developing a concrete advantage. He can, for example, find a niche and develop an advantage in it. He can also develop an original method and apply it on a regular basis. It is important to note that in the most important trading is not to find a revolutionary method to predict the evolution of stock prices, but simply to find a method with an interesting probability of success9 and to apply them on a regular basis. But often, traders will not respect their system and will be victims of their emotions. Differentiation consists in having an irreproachable preparation and developing a solid and efficient system.

The Emerging Strategy

This strategy does not question the two previous strategies. A trader can opt for global domination by cost or for differentiation and from time to time adopt an emerging strategy.

An emerging strategy can be defined as a strategy that arises from action. A trader can, for example, be bearish on the market and sell short several securities, then realize that the market holds, that it is not really bearish and that some elements point even in the direction of a bull market. The trader realizes that his idea of origin no longer works and his action [short sale] makes him realize that the markets are bullish. It will be able to be based on this observation and to place itself in the purchase.

To illustrate the concept of emerging strategy we are mentioning the experience of a financial author, from March 2000.

On March 26, 2000, I gave a lecture on the technical indicators at the Technical Analysis show in front of a sold-out room. My diagnosis on the NASDAQ was still bullish and I explained, showing the index graph, that there was currently no danger in this market which remained well oriented with an RSI above 50%. Nevertheless, the main risk was the presence of a bearish divergence not yet validated. If it were to be, we could see a bearish stall.

A few days later, Abby Joseph Cohen, chairman of the investment committee of Goldman Sachs explains "that it reduced from 70% to 65% the share of the shares in its standard portfolio, because of the recent rise of the courses". It was not necessarily bearish as it held 65% equities in its typical portfolio, but the sharp drop in markets validated the bearish divergence.

Then, I understood the issue and I realized that the market is really drawing a major reversal. Indeed, the bearish divergence on the NASDAQ was confirmed by other downward divergences validated on the main European stock market indices (CAC 40, Dax 30, etc.). I, therefore, went bearish on March 29, 2000, on the main indices IS & P 500, CAC 40, DAX 30, MIB ...] and I recommended my clients to sell their securities. This was certainly an emerging strategy since I relied on new elements that I did not have."

This example shows how important it is for a trader to be flexible and never stubborn. It's a good trader's job not to have a fixed opinion and to let the market behavior dictate what to do.

The Primary Goal of the Trader Must Be His Survival

According to Sun Tzu, one of the most important characteristics of the art of warfare is to make oneself invincible and never to take undue risks. Thus, the trader must aim above all for survival and closely monitor his exposure.

Manage Your Resources Well

The trader must win by saving himself. He must reserve himself for the best moments and avoid positioning himself simply to kill time. Sun Tzu expressed the same idea 2,500 years ago: "By calculation, consider whether the enemy can be attacked, and only then should the population be mobilized, and the troops lifted; learn how to distribute munitions of war and mouth always, never to give in the excesses of too much or too little."

According to Paul Tudor Jones "always thinking about what we will lose not that we will win, I never risk large amounts of money when figures are going to be released because it is a bet and more than trading."

By positioning the trader is comforted as it feels to be part of the game, but he does not realize he is about to sign financial death. This is the point of view of the great trader Larry Hite who claims not to be in the markets for excitement but to win. The trader should not afford to lose money on positions with a low probability of success. Indeed, it will not be in optimal conditions when the real opportunity will appear: he will be too afraid to position himself and will not open a position; he can take his courage with both hands and try. But in this case, his position will not be consistent because of previously recorded losses that have reduced his capital and therefore decreased his capacity for action.

Often, in trend-free markets, traders will lose lots of ammo and energy instead of booking for the most profitable times (trend markets for example). So when the real movement starts, it's already too late. Much of their capital has been decimated and they no longer have the psychological strength to participate in the movement.

Never Measure Yourself against Yourself

For Sun Tzu, we must avoid attacking the fortresses and prefer to put the enemy strategies at risk because they are much more malleable. Always wait for the best time to position yourself, never before. The markets are always right and the trader must avoid any ego or seek to impose his point of view on them.

Stay Discreet About Your Intentions

"The great art of a general is to make sure that the enemy is always ignorant of the place where he will have to fight and to carefully remove from him the knowledge of the posts he keeps. If he comes to the end and can conceal even the least of his steps, he is not only a skillful general; he is an extraordinary man, a prodigy. Without being seen, he sees; he hears without being heard; he acts noiselessly and disposes of as he pleases the fate of his enemies." – Sun Tzu.

The trader has every interest in being discreet about his intentions. This idea applies perfectly to institutional traders. Indeed, if a particular trader is not likely to move the markets due to limited capital, an institutional trader because of its significant positions can quickly be spotted by other operators. Therefore, it is in his best interest to remain discreet about his intentions and never open his position in a single time. Often, important traders split their positions so as not to let their intentions show through.

If for example, a trader wants to get rid of a million titles, this operation will cause a sharp decline in the title if it is performed at once, which will result in an unfavorable average selling price. It is therefore in the interest of the trader not to declare his plans and remain discreet in the way he operates.

Some big traders claim to mentally place their stops so that they are not known by their competitors since some traders can quite easily get this information from brokers and take advantage of it.

The Interest of Never Revealing Its Strategy

"Let the enemy never know how you intend to fight him, nor how you will attack him, or defend yourself. For if he prepares for the front, his rear will be weak; if he gets ready in the back, his forehead will be fragile; if he prepares on his left, his right will be vulnerable; if he prepares on his right, his left will be weakened; and if he prepares himself everywhere, he will be everywhere in default. If he absolutely ignores it, he will make great preparations, he will try to make himself strong on all sides, he will divide his forces, and that is precisely what will make his loss." – Sun Tzu.

The trader should not make the task easy for his competitors by revealing strategic information. It is better to leave a doubt about one's intentions and wait for the error to come from others. Like chess or poker, you have to have nerves of steel to succeed in trading.

A Preparation without Flaws

Attack and defense techniques must be mastered by traders. Nevertheless, they must be supplemented by solid preparation. The best traders spend a lot of time preparing for them. They know the markets in which they operate their competitors and have powerful tools.

Know Your Environment

Sun Tzu insists enormously on the importance of preparation: "Consider that with many calculations one can win the victory, fear their inadequacy. It is thanks to this method that I examine the situation, and the outcome will be clear. Before coming to a final battle, you must have foreseen it, and have been prepared for a long time; never rely on chance in everything you do in this way. Anticipate everything, dispose of everything, and rely on the enemy when he still believes you a hundred leagues away."

The trader must be familiar with the markets in which it will work (rhythmic, historical development, key support and resistance levels, indicators work best, etc.). He will also have to identify the false signals generated on this market.

The Importance of Preparation

The trader must take care to establish a solid strategy and to set himself the entry levels, the main pivots, the levels on which profit-taking can be made, the levels around which he can increase his position, cut his position, etc. Before opening a position, the trader is able to determine when he is going to strengthen it, as well as the circumstances that will lead him to take his profits or simply get out of his position. He has already

169

visualized multiple scenarios and mentally prepared for their occurrence. Jean Brilman declines the four-step strategy that we will apply to trade.

Analyzing the Situation

First of all, the strategist must know his business and the initial situation. The OM / FF model (also known as SWOT) of the Harvard School (strengths/weaknesses, opportunities/threats) recommends that the strategist perform an analysis to assess his strengths and weaknesses, and also, to identify in its environment the main opportunities and threats. The objective of the strategy is above all to develop a sustainable and sustainable competitive advantage.

The trader will have to proceed in the same way by controlling his environment, that is to say by having a perfect knowledge of his main competitors. He will also have to determine his strengths and weaknesses, i.e. the financial means he says, his analytical skills, his trading skills as well as the skills he will have to acquire and develop in the future.

Specialize

After the preliminary analysis of the situation, the trader will have to determine the market on which he intends to operate (equities, currencies, futures, options, etc.), which method will be used (technical analysis, fundamental analysis, analysis order book, etc.) and finally the time horizon (short term, medium term, long term). This decision will depend heavily on the analysis of the situation, his skills and the means at its disposal.

Develop a Competitive Advantage

The trader will seek to develop a competitive advantage based on the means at his disposal and his skills. A particular trader will avoid difficult markets and sophisticated techniques and will specialize in medium-term investment. A well-capitalized institutional trader with the most up-to-date technology and very favorable terms from his brokers will be able to specialize in short-term trading.

Beyond this specialization, each trader will have to identify a niche, that is to say, adopt a technique tested on a long enough history and generating positive profitability. It must also be certain that the implementation of this strategy gives it an undeniable advantage over its competitors.

Deploy Strategy

This step represents the implementation of the strategy. The trader can only start it if the three steps mentioned above have been carefully carried out. Deploying the strategy requires the trader to have a flawless discipline and a good knowledge of his psychological traits.

The strategy is not an exact science. The trader must essentially aim to develop an advantage over the competition and strive to implement it optimally on the markets. For this, it can use methods such as technical analysis or fundamental analysis and look for low-risk and profitable configurations. Its strategy will have to be tested on a long enough history and prove its veracity to be retained.

Who Are Our Competitors?

Every trader has to list his enemies or potential competitors. Who are they? What can be their impact? How to minimize their impact?

In each market, the competitors are different and arise where we least expect it. Moreover, the competitors are not necessarily located on the markets and can be for example time-consuming elements (meetings with repetition, information sparse and not enough centered on the essential, etc.). The trader will have to identify his competitors but also learn to better control his emotions to operate effectively in the markets.

The goal of the trader is to shelter while waiting for others to make mistakes. He must in no case succumb to the error of exposing himself. For a trader, the enemies are the portfolio managers, investors, brokers, and himself ... By controlling his main enemies, he puts on his side every chance to succeed.

Be Ready To Fight

"May your principal forces be all on the same side; if you want to attack head-on, make a choice of a sector, and put at the head of your troops all that you have of the best. One rarely resists a first effort, as, on the contrary, it is difficult to recover when one first from below. The example of the brave is enough to encourage your cowards. They follow without difficulty the path shown to them, but they cannot themselves spawn it. If you want to give the left-wing, turn all your preparations on that side, and put on the right-wing what you have weaker; but if you want to conquer by the right-wing, let it be on the right-wing as well as your best troops and all your attention." – Sun Tzu.

Gary Bielfeldt does not believe in diversification. His philosophy is to say that you have to specialize in one area and become an expert. The most important thing for a trader is to have a method to keep his winning positions and get rid of his losing positions quickly.

Specialization is of paramount importance in trading, especially the early days. Novice traders tend to want to do too much at the beginning and disperse. The losses they suffered forced them to give up while a specialization at the beginning would have allowed them to limit the damage.

Too much information kills information: do not scatter. Some traders want to know everything about everything. They think that by having the most sophisticated instruments, the best software, they will be able to conquer the markets. Nothing is further from reality. In fact, the best traders have simple systems that they master perfectly. They know that by wanting too sophisticated things they risk losing their discipline and taking unfavorable positions.

Visualization

Great traders are used to visualizing their different tactics before markets open. They imagine themselves operating and mentally repeating the most appropriate movements. When markets open, they are already ready.

Mental training trader allows him to be ready and condition when the markets open. He has in mind what he is supposed to do in this or that situation. His strategies must be fully assimilated and mastered so that he can react almost instinctively to situations. Like the general, he must be prepared for the most catastrophic scenarios. The trader must be prepared to act in situations where everything turns against him and be ready for the unexpected.

He knows his weaknesses well and does everything to limit their negative impact. A day trader who loves action should be vigilant during quiet market phases because he may be bored, which will incite him to initiate positions impulsively.

Cunning

Many traders will forget about any trading plan and let their decisions be dictated by the markets. For Sun Tzu, it's important not to let the game take you and take the lead.

"There will be occasions when you will lower, and others where you will affect to be afraid. You will sometimes pretend to be weak, so that your enemies, opening the door to presumption and pride, will come to attack you improperly or allow themselves to be surprised and cut to pieces shamefully. You will make it so that those who are inferior to you can never penetrate your designs. You will keep your troops always alert, always in

175

motion and in occupation, to prevent them from being softened by a shameful rest. "

Cunning: The Art of Manipulating Opponents to One's Advantage

In the financial markets, there is no need for manipulation since traders fall into the trap of their psychological biases. They often have a poor understanding of the financial markets and rush when to wait and wait to take action. Sometimes, some traders will seek to provoke these reactions by for example breaking support or resistance so as to trigger an emotional reaction in their competitors.

The best traders know how to use the psychological bias of other traders for their benefit. They have studied their attitudes and are able to guess how they will behave in certain situations. Thus, they will voluntarily provoke these psychological biases to obtain desired effects among novice traders that they can use for their benefit. They are inspired by that of Sun Tzu.

"The great science is to make him want anything you want him to do, and to provide him, without his noticing it, all the means to assist you."

This is for the trader to decide when the transition to action should begin. Nothing must be imposed on him. Thus, a trader can artificially raise prices to create a certain euphoria among

176

traders and encourage them to position themselves for the purchase. Conversely, in a bear market, professional traders will have an interest in exacerbating the fears of novices.

In trading, this means that the trader must use the psychological bias of others to his advantage instead of being a victim. The trader should never rush and make sure his competitors work for him. He waits for the best moment before positioning himself, that is to say, the one where the other traders make mistakes, victims of their impatience. In a market without trend, it is not uncommon to note many false breaks support or resistance.

Fulcrums and Turns

An upper pivot point is the highest point of a price movement before the low of the highest bar is broken down. A lower pivot point is the lowest point of a price movement before the high of the lowest bar is breached upwards. An upper fulcrum becomes a resistance, a lower fulcrum becomes support. The movement from one fulcrum to the next is called momentum.

The Direction of the Trend

The trend rises as long as new highs and higher lows are reached. The shift to the downtrend occurs when the last low before the highest high is breached.

Closing Prices

A number of close-out prices within a relatively small range indicate a market that is in a state of equilibrium. Moving away from this close range of close prices suggests an imbalance where demand exceeds supply or vice versa. On the basis of this assumption, patterns can be developed with which one obtains a technical advantage when dealing with the trend. Be very careful if you want to use such patterns as an entry point against the prevailing trend. You can minimize the risk by making a correction after the closing price points the way.

A two-bar closing price reversal with increased spread is likely to signal a significant reversal when it occurs in the direction of the trend. The odds increase when the closing price is below the end of the previous bar.

If several closing prices occur within a narrow range, then the last closing price often indicates the direction in which the breakout will occur from this equilibrium. If the first thrust comes from a close formation of several closeouts with a long bar, then it usually points in the direction the course will take in the short term.

Closing Prices with Non-Overlapping Bars

An even weaker pattern is a three-bar pattern with a non-overlapping bar - a bar whose height is below the bottom of the last bar with the top pivot point.

The Direction of the Trend

A bar running against the direction of the four previous final curves may indicate a trend reversal. If the four closing prices are close to each other and not all rising, then the trend changes to the bottom. If all four closing prices are rising, then the reverse bar is likely to correct only the overbought situation and the shift is neutral.

Once the course has reached its goal, the profits can be protected as follows:

1. Close the position upon reaching the target course

2. Tracing a stop at least three ticks below the lows of each bar

3. Set a stop a tick below a correction that corresponds to the extent of the previous correction

4. Hold the position until a four-bar reversal occurs

5. Closing the position if higher closing prices occur over three or four bars

6. Closing the position when reverse patterns occur in the next shorter time frame

This is often an indication of the validity of the breakthrough. It is generally statistically significant and gives a small advantage to the trader if the previous bar shows signs of demand closing above the opening price (point 3 above). However, this advantage is not enough to make up for the slippage and day trading fees. You could do more research by keeping a profitable position longer and securing it with a tight stop. This is how successful trading systems are developed.

Reversal Day

A reversal day signals a one-day change from the bulls to the bears or vice versa. From a statistical point of view, this pattern alone cannot be used profitably, but in combination with other technical indicators, it can be very useful.

A reversal day is a day on which a value trades below (above) the pre-tort rate and then closes above (below) the low (high) and opening price of the previous day. This type of price movement may mean a temporary or permanent end to a smaller prevailing trend.

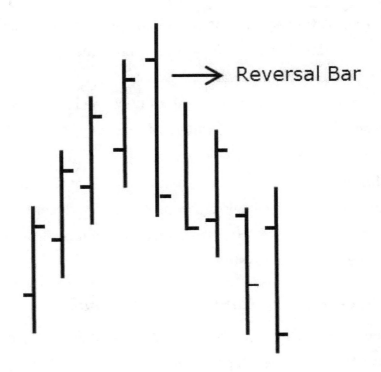

Reversal Bar

Type and Occurrence of the Reversal Days

The following factors influence the meaning of a reversal day:

1. The span of the beam

2. The number of closing prices that are reversed

3. The number of pivot points that are above and below

Using computers, the reverse tag pattern was tested for its suitability as a market entry. The following filters have been added:

1. Buy / Sell at the end of the day on which the simple round-trip day is trained.

2. Exit: After the opening of the position, the exit takes place on the first day on which the price opens higher or lower by 50% of the previous day's spread.

3. Trend filter: A purchase will only be made if the previous day closes above 50 days ago (and vice versa).

The use of the reverse-day pattern has a significant technical advantage. Nevertheless, the profit is insufficient to cover the fees and slippage. However, further attempts could lead to a successful trading system.

Three-Day Balance and Reversal

The price movements of the last three days often point in the direction of the next small step.

The strongest three-day equilibrium (3DE) reversal occurs when the high and close of the current day are above the high of the previous two days and the closing price is higher than the opening price. Negative reversal is the opposite. This pattern occurs approximately 35 to 40 times a year in equities and futures. One way to successfully use this pattern is to wait one day and buy it at the closing price of the following day.

Conclusion

Thank you for making it through to the end of *Options Trading 1*, let's hope it was informative and able to provide you with all of the tools you need to achieve your goals whatever they may be.

Concluding a book is not easy because a book is never a culmination but first and foremost a beginning. This first step traveled together is nevertheless the most important in our training (or your development) because it aims at access to knowledge. Trading, like any other activity, can be learned, and this is what we have tried to show by bringing many theoretical arguments, but also drawn from the practice to support our remarks.

I hope that our goal has been achieved and that the apprentice trader now has a reference book to better understand the financial markets, to anticipate movements in stock prices but also to develop successful strategies to capitalize on inefficiencies steps. I hope I have convinced you that trading was above all an art and not a science and that success in this area was possible if the trader agrees to make the necessary efforts. As in any activity, the trader will have to successfully complete several stages before being able to claim the title of master in trading.

My second objective was to prove the effectiveness of the technical analysis, so often decried in the academic world, and to improve its image by providing solid arguments. Over the course of my professional career, I have made many successful forecasts thanks to this approach and I found it unjust that it is not yet considered worthy. I hope that other people in France, and elsewhere, will take up the torch and will try to enrich the results in this book in terms of stock market analysis and strategy. I would also like to acknowledge the remarkable work done by the French Association of Technical Analysts and its senior leaders in promoting this approach.

Today, market access is easy. Anyone can have quick, real-time access to major exchanges around the world, 24 hours a day. In addition, you do not have to be a full-time employee. To stay in front of your computers continuously (except for day traders). Modern technologies allow us to place electronic orders that will perform for us various tasks (profit-taking, exit a title when a certain threshold has been depressed). However, if the physical presence in front of the screen is not necessary, the trader will not be able to save a lot of preparatory work. Indeed, this ease of access is a double-edged sword. Having analytical tools no longer means a decisive advantage in the markets. During my seminars, I met people who performed spectacularly and who lost everything as a result of an opposing movement. Trading is not an easy activity and I have tried in this book to provide many "strings" that I consider important to survive at first, then to succeed for the most enduring. These remarks are not intended to discourage you, but rather to prepare you mentally for the hard task ahead. Success in trading is possible but it is not easy.

Trading is an activity that requires many psychological qualities, which most people do not have: only those who are able to control their emotions can capitalize on the emotions of others and therefore their mistakes, which explains the existence of opportunities recurring on the markets. A good trader must have foolproof patience, a real will and a good dose of humility. Finally, it is a solitary job where one is alone to savor one's victories and one cannot blame others for his mistakes. This loneliness is also posed as one of the conditions for success by many high-flying traders. This aspect of trading activity may seem tricky in a society where one only exists through one's status and where socialization goes through work. Nevertheless, the situation seems to be changing in the 21st century. We are immersed in an economy of knowledge and knowledge where remote work is becoming more and more widespread. Trading is undeniably a profession of the future for perfectly prepared people.

In this book, I strived to show that trading is not a natural process and requires specific qualities. I am talking here about private traders operating for their personal account from home, and non-professional swing traders who are in a stimulating environment. Sometimes, some traders organize themselves into a group to work together in the same trading room. This is sometimes a good thing when there is coherence in the group and real support. And I hope this book finds you in the best of spirits, and by this time, you would be raring to go, learn, practice and win.

Finally, if you found this book useful in any way, a review on Amazon is always appreciated!